ZAPiro

Don't Mess With the President's Head

Cartoons from *Mail & Guardian*, *Sunday Times* and *The Times*

JACANA

Acknowledgements: Thanks to my editors at the Mail & Guardian
(Nic Dawes, Ferial Haffajee), at the Sunday Times *(Mondli Makhanya)*
and at The Times *(Ray Hartley) and the production staff at all
the newspapers; my assistants Alecia Hartmann and Lisa Stemmet;
Bridget Impey, Russell Martin and all at Jacana; Claudine Willatt-Bate;
Nomalizo Ndlazi; and my family: Tevya, Nina and my wife Karina.*

10 Orange Street
Sunnyside
Auckland Park 2092
South Africa
(+27 11) 628-3200
www.jacana.co.za

in association with

©2009 Jonathan Shapiro

ISBN 978-1-77009-757-5

Cover design by Jonathan Shapiro

Page layout by Claudine Willatt-Bate
Printed by Creda Communications
Job No. 1073

See a complete list of Jacana titles at www.jacana.co.za

For the Arch

Other ZAPIRO books

The Madiba Years (1996)

The Hole Truth (1997)

End of Part One (1998)

Call Mr Delivery (1999)

The Devil Made Me Do It! (2000)

The ANC Went in 4x4 (2001)

Bushwhacked (2002)

Dr Do-Little and the African Potato (2003)

Long Walk to Free Time (2004)

Is There a Spin Doctor In the House? (2005)

Da Zuma Code (2006)

Take Two Veg and Call Me In the Morning (2007)

Pirates of Polokwane (2008)

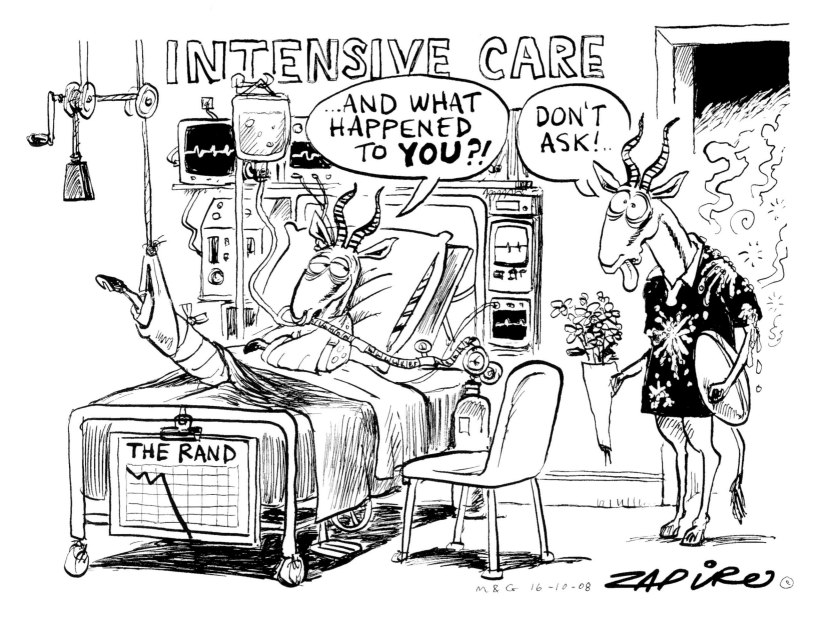

16 October 2008

Global market crash. Player Luke Watson says rugby's failure to transform makes him want to vomit on his Springbok jersey.

5

Insults as senior cadres follow Mosiuoa Lekota and Mbhazima Shilowa out.
The 'elitist cigar-smoking whiskey-drinking counter-revolutionaries' say
it's ANC leaders themselves who've undermined party principles.

19 October 2008

23 October 2008

Playing down resignations of national exec members,
provincial premiers and scores of regional leaders

30 October 2008

Halloween marks the eve of US elections. Republican Senator
John McCain has Sarah Palin as his breathtakingly ignorant running mate.

1 November 2008   Inspirational Democratic Senator Barack Obama holds a solid lead

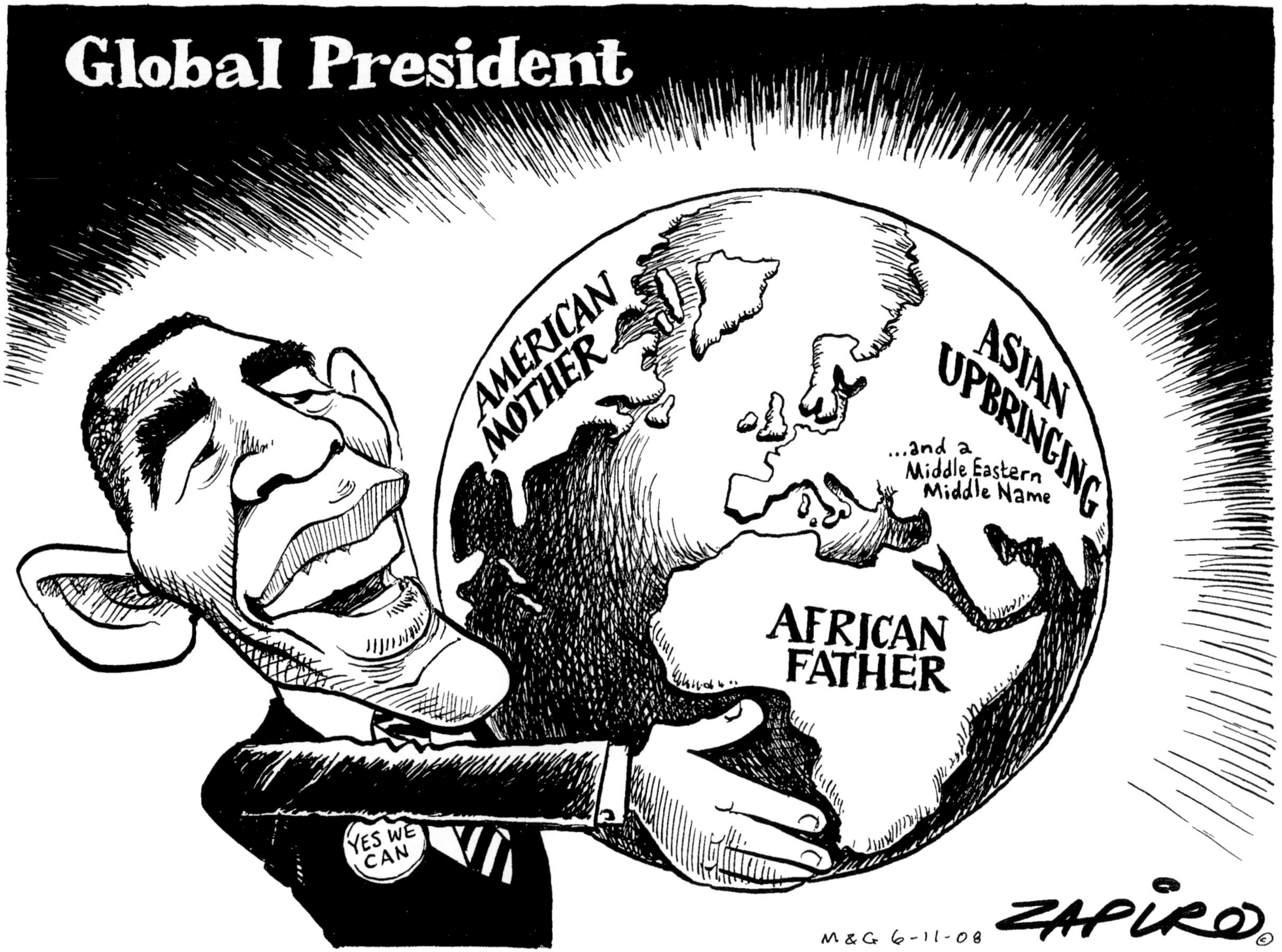
Global President
AMERICAN MOTHER
ASIAN UPBRINGING
...and a Middle Eastern Middle Name
AFRICAN FATHER
YES WE CAN
M&G 6-11-08
ZAPIRO ©

6 November 2008

Clear winner

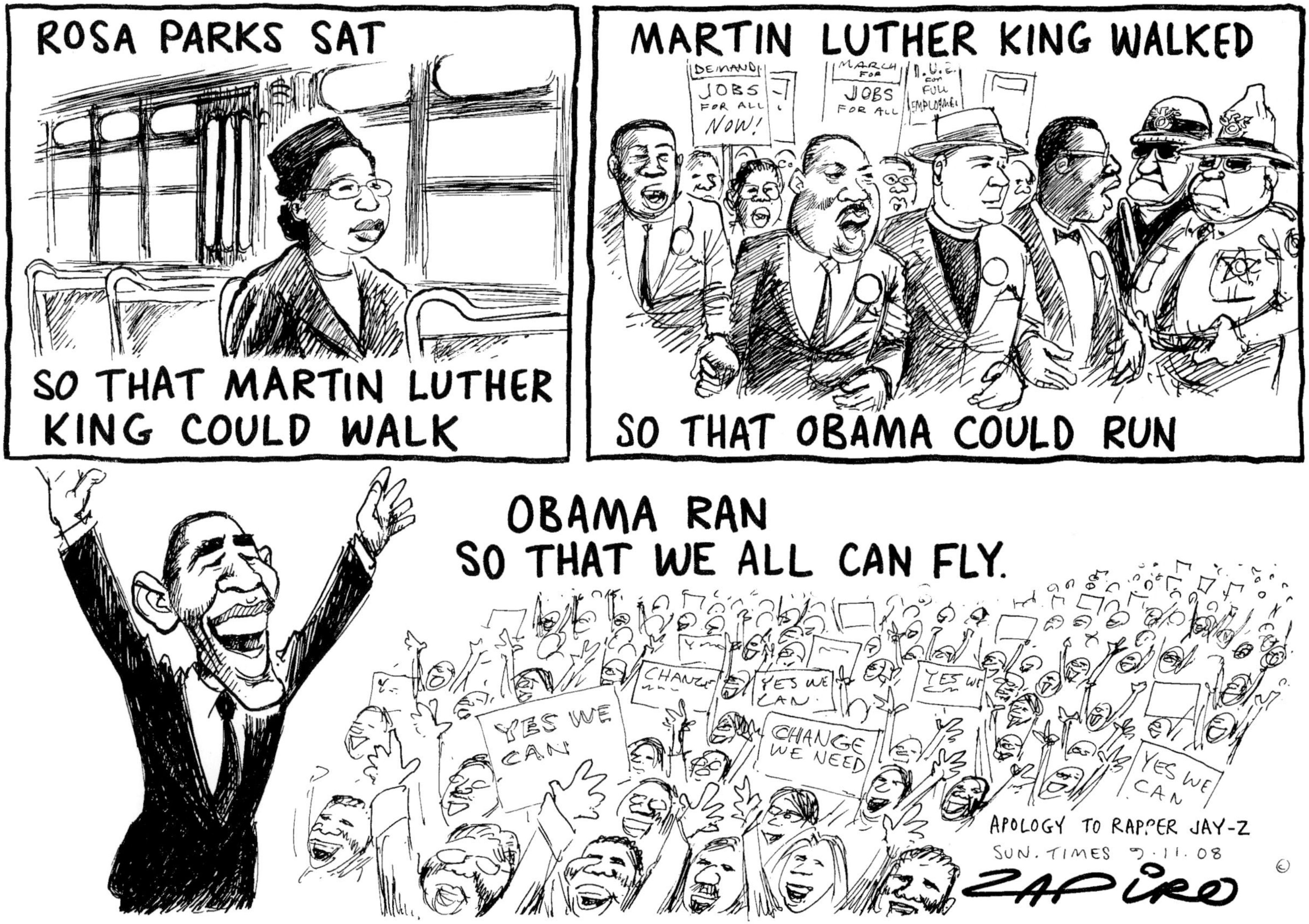
ROSA PARKS SAT
SO THAT MARTIN LUTHER KING COULD WALK
MARTIN LUTHER KING WALKED
DEMAND JOBS FOR ALL NOW!
MARCH FOR JOBS FOR ALL
SO THAT OBAMA COULD RUN
OBAMA RAN SO THAT WE ALL CAN FLY.
CHANGE
YES WE CAN
YES WE
YES WE CAN
CHANGE WE NEED
YES WE CAN
APOLOGY TO RAPPER JAY-Z
SUN. TIMES 9.11.08
ZAPIRO
©

9 November 2008

MAMA
AFRICA
Miriam Makeba
1932–2008

ZAPIRO

© M&G 13-11-08

13 November 2008

16 November 2008

Shilowa and Lekota plan their launch, facing animal insults
and an ANC court challenge to their new party's name

20 November 2008   Can Julius Malema be reined in without alienating the Youth League he heads?

Then there's the off-the-cuff pronouncements of the party's top man

The Council for Scientific and Industrial Research (CSIR)
suspends a top researcher for announcing his damaging findings

27 November 2008

30 November 2008   80 dead as Islamist gunmen attack tourist spots in Mumbai, India

New party claiming moral high ground

Suspended prosecutions head Vusi Pikoli, cleared by a commission of inquiry, is axed
by President Kgalema Motlanthe, who also rejects renewed calls for an arms deal probe

11 December 2008

14 December 2008

… living up to his 'caretaker president' tag

In cholera-stricken Zimbabwe, power-sharing mediator Mbeki is accused
of still favouring Mugabe. Meanwhile a Harvard study claims Mbeki's
domestic Aids policy caused 330 000 preventable deaths.

7 December 2008

18 December 2008

At a news conference in Baghdad, an Iraqi
journalist throws his shoes at President George W Bush

22

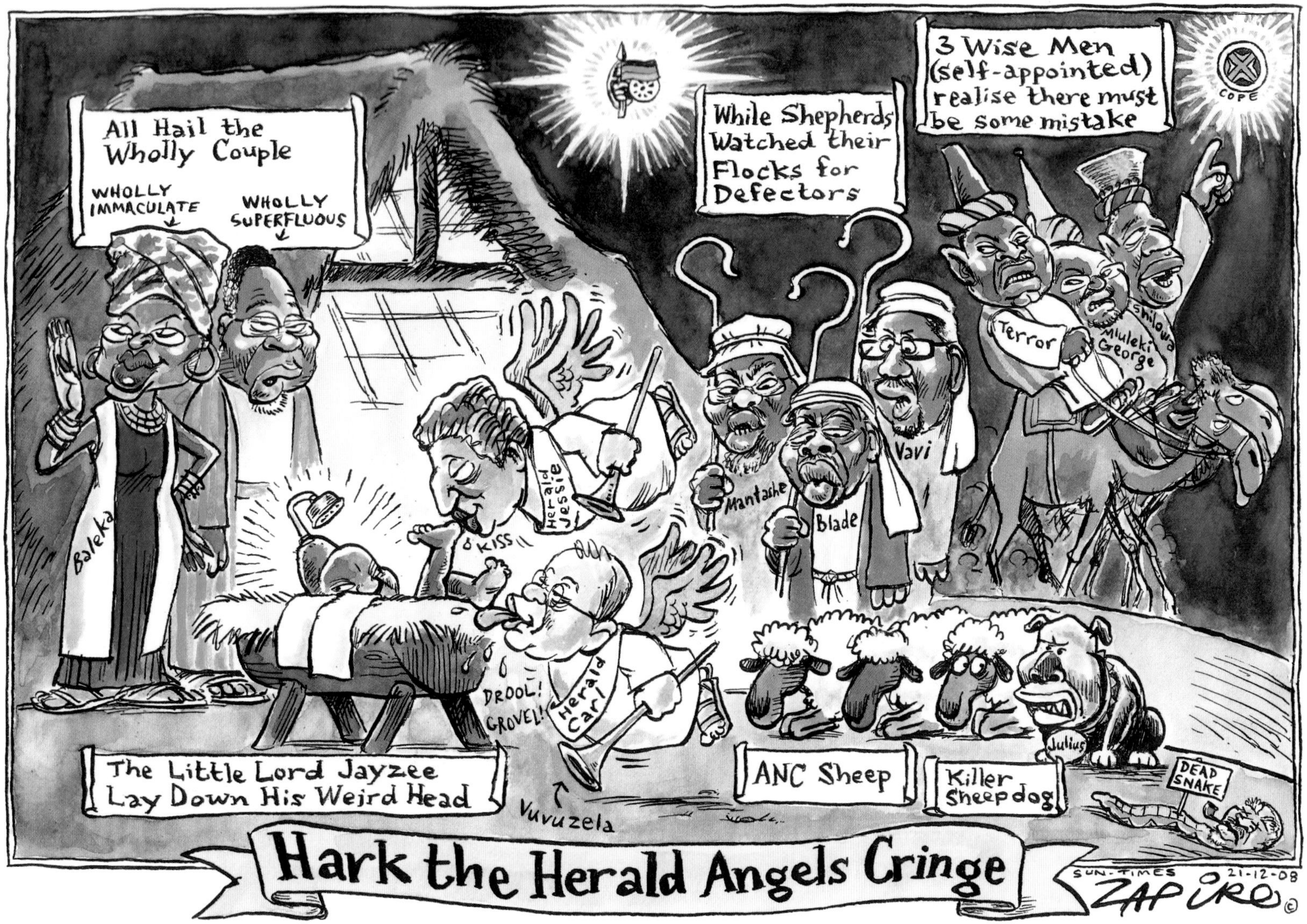
All Hail the Wholly Couple
WHOLLY IMMACULATE
WHOLLY SUPERFLUOUS
Baleka
While Shepherds Watched their Flocks for Defectors
3 Wise Men (self-appointed) realise there must be some mistake
COPE
Terror
Mluleki George
Shilowa
Mantashe
Blade
Vavi
Herald Jessie
O KISS
Herald Carl
DROOL! GROVEL!
The Little Lord Jayzee Lay Down His Weird Head
Vuvuzela
ANC Sheep
Killer Sheepdog
Julius
DEAD SNAKE
Hark the Herald Angels Cringe
SUN-TIMES 21-12-08
ZAPIRO ©

21 December 2008

11 January 2009

Already crippled by an 18-month siege, Gaza is pounded by missiles that
kill hundreds of civilians. Israel cites cross-border Hamas rockets as provocation.

ZAPIRO M&G 15-1-09

15 January 2009

Slating Judge Nicholson's High Court ruling that dismissed corruption
charges against Zuma, the Supreme Court of Appeal reinstates the charges

18 January 2009

Ahead of the US presidential inauguration

23 January 2009   Promise of hope and change

27

25 January 2009

His soaring rhetoric has invoked great statesmen

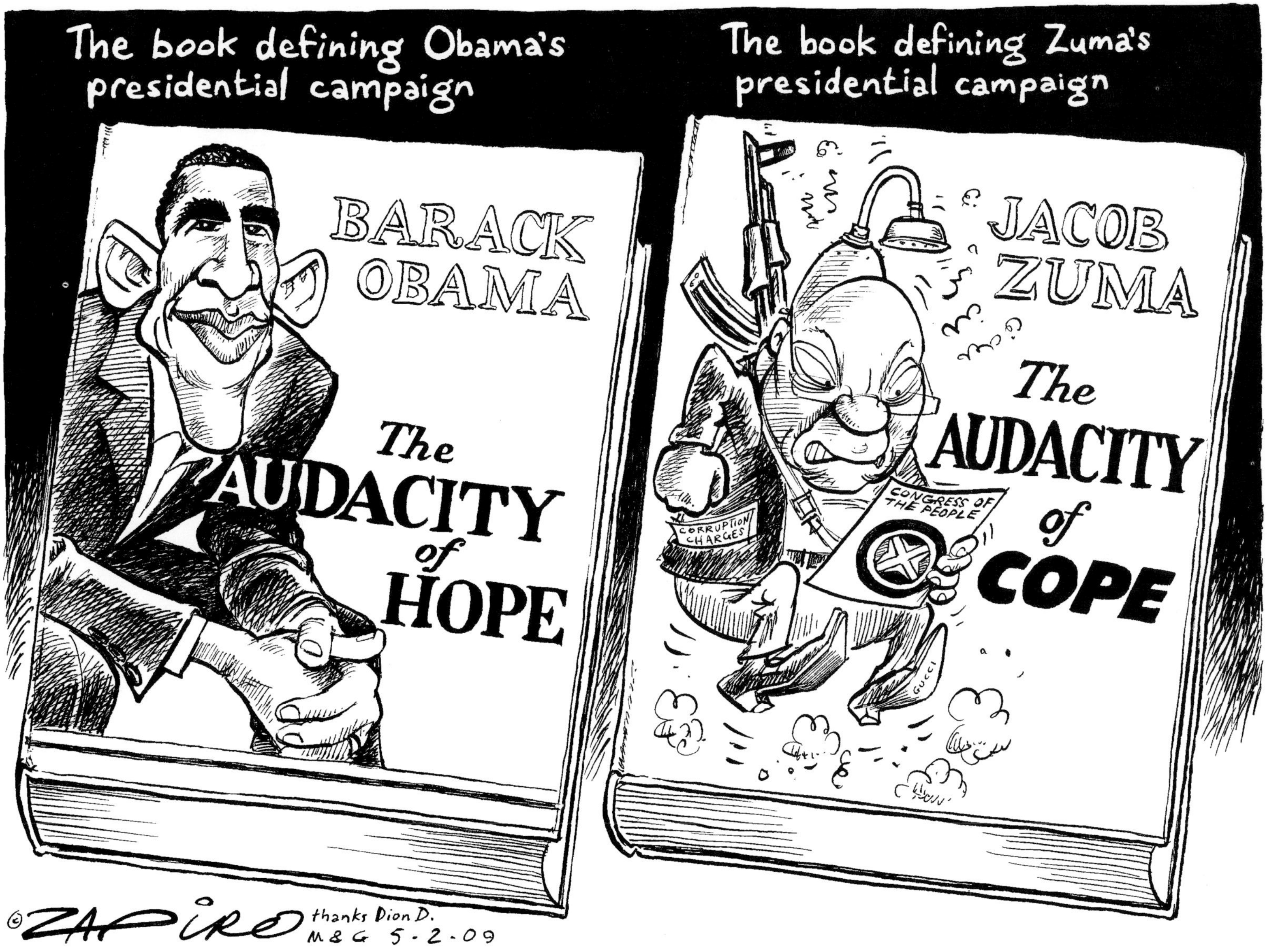
The book defining Obama's presidential campaign
BARACK OBAMA
The AUDACITY of HOPE
The book defining Zuma's presidential campaign
JACOB ZUMA
The AUDACITY of COPE
CORRUPTION CHARGES
CONGRESS OF THE PEOPLE
GUCCI
©ZAPIRO thanks Dion D. M&G 5-2-09

5 February 2009

8 February 2009

Awkward event for five-month presidential
bench-warmer ahead of keenly anticipated general election

30

12 February 2009

Loosening of Mugabe's 29-year grip on power as his
long-time rival Morgan Tsvangirai becomes prime minister

Finally losing it with Julius Malema, the ANC makes him write an apology to Naledi Pandor, the cabinet minister he insulted. And ANC national spokesman Carl Niehaus is exposed, tearfully admitting to bad debts, lies and forgery.

15 February 2009

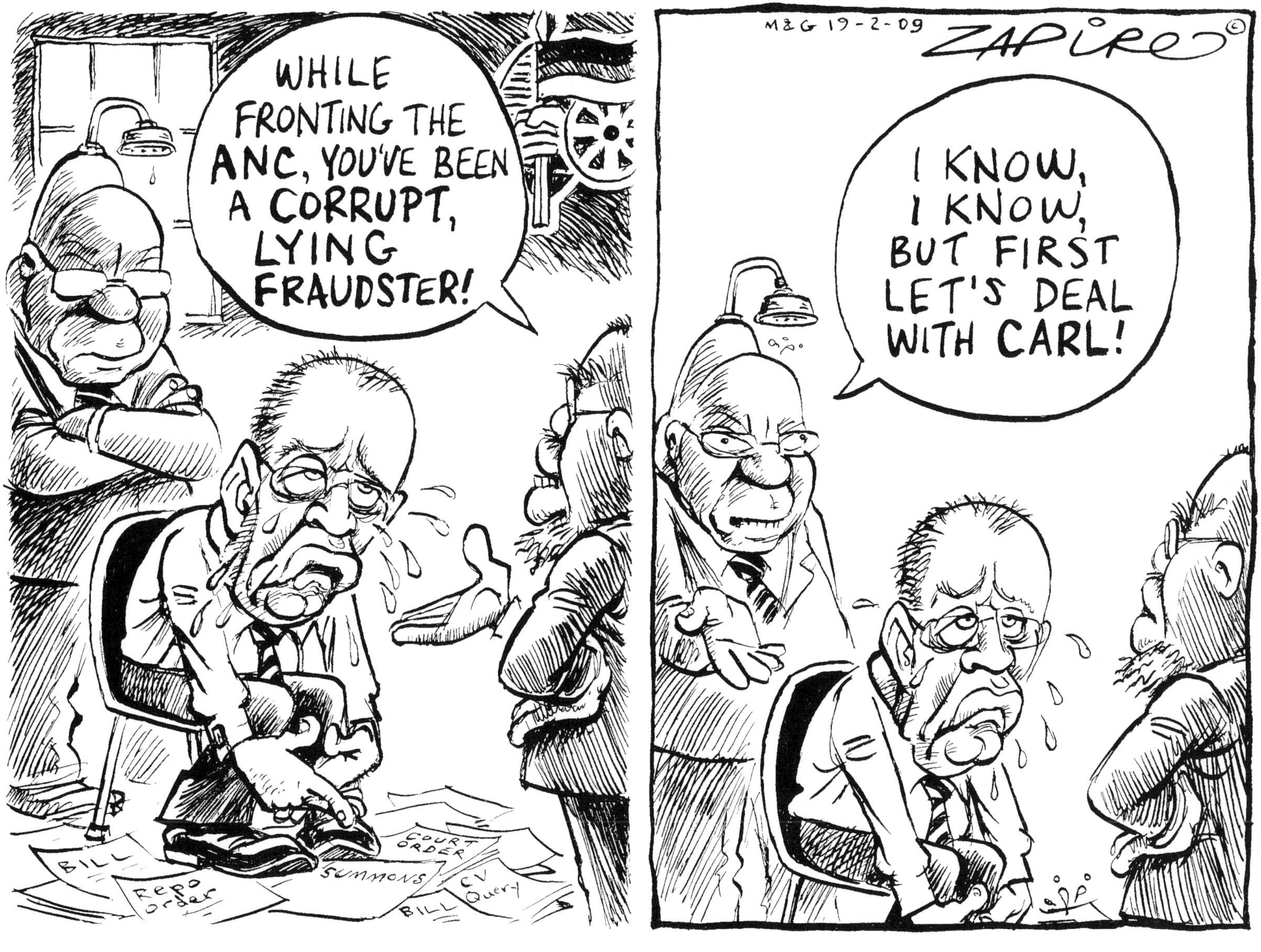
WHILE FRONTING THE ANC, YOU'VE BEEN A CORRUPT, LYING FRAUDSTER!
BILL
Repo order
SUMMONS
COURT ORDER
CV Query
BILL
M&G 19-2-09
ZAPIRO ©
I KNOW, I KNOW, BUT FIRST LET'S DEAL WITH CARL!

19 February 2009

Election list topped by the presidential hopeful facing corruption
charges and peppered with candidates facing charges or with fraud records

22 February 2009

DEPT OF CONNECTIONAL SERVICES
PAROLE BOARD

PAROLE APPLICANT: Schabir Shaik

MOTIVATION:

"Schabir Shaik is corrupt"
— Judge Squires 2006

"Corruption is a terrible sickness of society"
— Jacob Zuma 2007

therefore:
Schabir Shaik is terribly sick.

MEDICAL PAROLE: REFUSED ☐   GRANTED ☑

He suffers from hypertension, but is he 'terminally ill'? Outcry when he's released after serving a quarter of his 15-year sentence for corruption involving Zuma.

5 March 2009

35

Early factional tensions between COPE president Lekota and deputy Shilowa.
Former cleric Mvume Dandala brought in out of nowhere to be presidential candidate.

26 February 2009

36

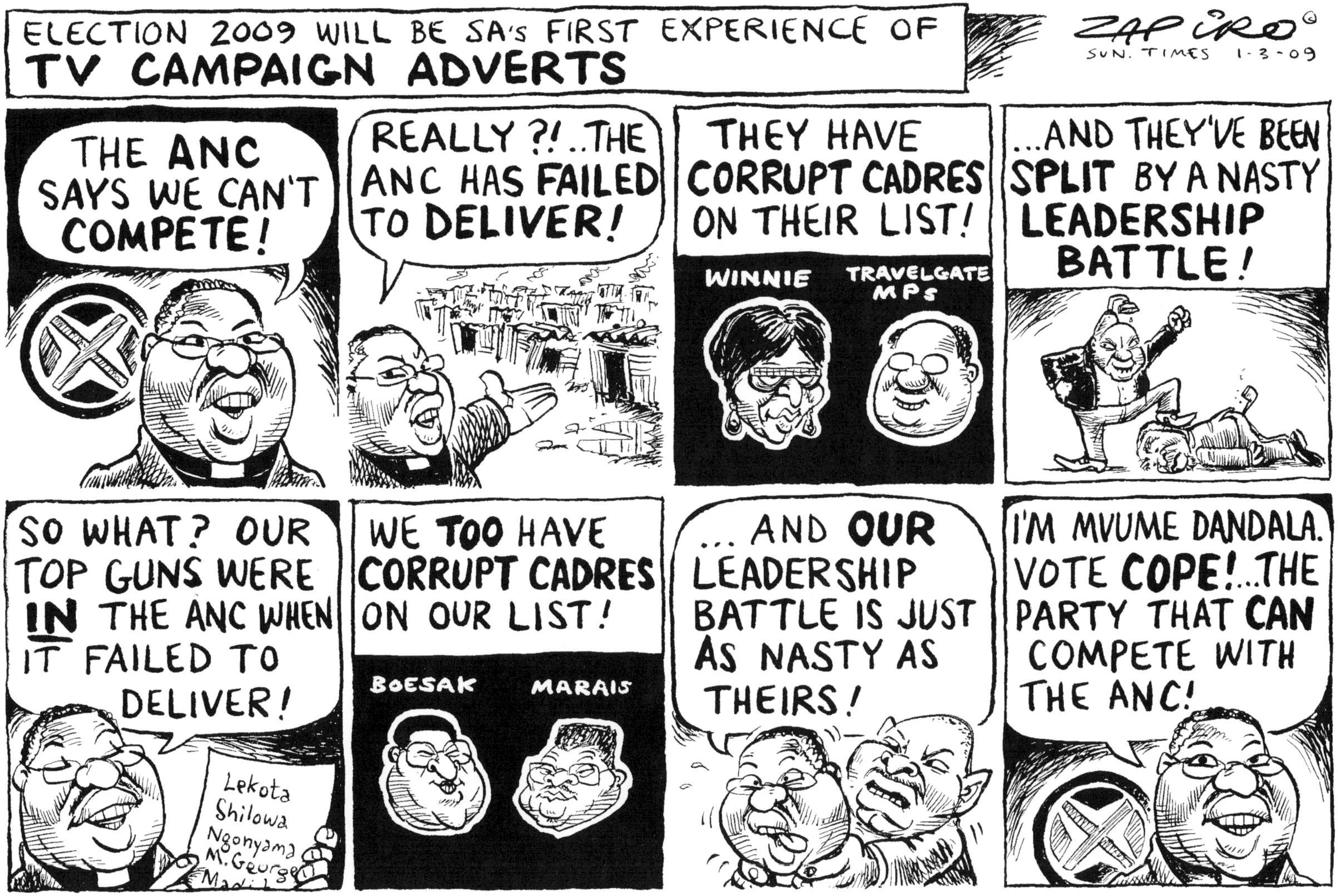
ELECTION 2009 WILL BE SA's FIRST EXPERIENCE OF
TV CAMPAIGN ADVERTS
ZAPIRO ©
SUN. TIMES 1-3-09
THE ANC SAYS WE CAN'T COMPETE!
REALLY ?! ..THE ANC HAS FAILED TO DELIVER!
THEY HAVE CORRUPT CADRES ON THEIR LIST!
WINNIE
TRAVELGATE MPs
...AND THEY'VE BEEN SPLIT BY A NASTY LEADERSHIP BATTLE!
SO WHAT? OUR TOP GUNS WERE IN THE ANC WHEN IT FAILED TO DELIVER!
Lekota
Shilowa
Ngonyama
M.George
WE TOO HAVE CORRUPT CADRES ON OUR LIST!
BOESAK
MARAIS
... AND OUR LEADERSHIP BATTLE IS JUST AS NASTY AS THEIRS!
I'M MVUME DANDALA. VOTE COPE!...THE PARTY THAT CAN COMPETE WITH THE ANC!

1 March 2009

8 March 2009

In Lahore, Pakistan, terrorist gunmen thought to be linked to the recent
attacks in India attack the Sri Lankan cricket team's tour bus, killing eight people

The CEO who's been suspended for nepotism involving
his wife's business deals is finally axed, with big payout

11 March 2009

14 March 2009

When Morgan Tsvangirai's wife dies in a mysterious car crash, some suspect foul play. At her memorial service, Mugabe advances a different theory.

ELECTION 2009: THE *slightly edited* PARTY SLOGANS

M&G 19-3-09 ZAPIRO

IFP — THE T(ir)RIED AND de TESTED ALTERNATIVE

UDM — THE TIME IS NOW! ...or maybe later

PAC — LIBERATE AZANIA. SERVE THE(r)E PEOPLE!

ID — BE A PART from OF THE SOLUTION

ACDP — NEW HEART, NEW NATION — no brain required

AZAPO — FOR THE SAKE OF OUR COUNTRY vote any other party

MINORITY FRONT — STAND UP AND BE COUNTED — both of you!

FREEDOM FRONT + Plus VF — STAND UP FOR A BETTER ~~DISPENSATION~~ view

DA — ONE NATION, ONE(s) FUTURE — botox for the well-heeled

COPE — A *used* ~~NEW~~ AGENDA FOR CHANGE ~~AND HOPE!~~ —what

ANC — ...AND THERE'S THE FAMOUS... WORKING TOGETHER WE CAN DO MORE crime corruption nepotism cronyism etc. ANC A BETTER LIE FOR ALL

19 March 2009

One month to go

41

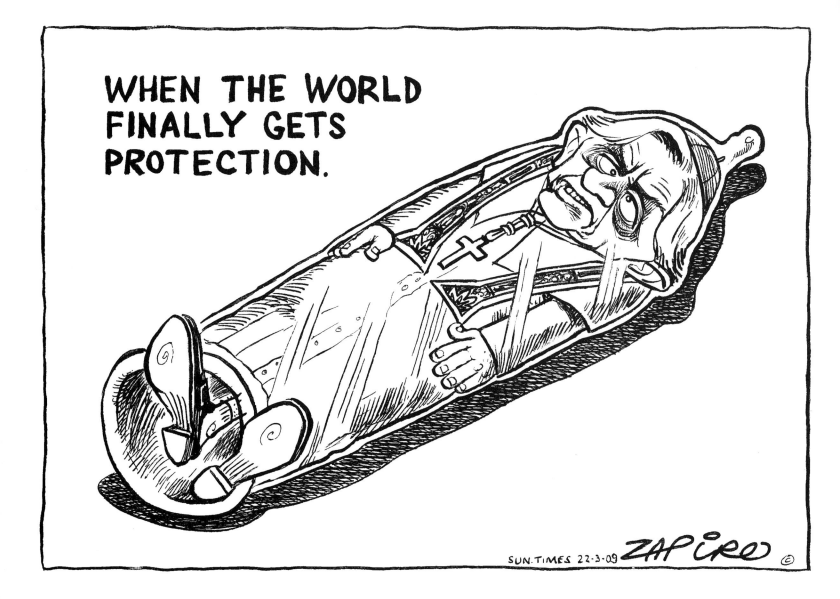

WHEN THE WORLD FINALLY GETS PROTECTION.

SUN.TIMES 22·3·09 ZAPIRO ©

22 March 2009

Visiting Africa where 22 million people live with HIV,
Pope Benedict says condoms won't help and can make the problem worse

SUN. TIMES
5-4-09 © ZAPIRO After Edward Linley Sambourne's "The Rhodes Colossus" (1892)

5 April 2009

As hosts of next year's World Cup we're avoiding conflict, says government as it refuses the Dalai Lama a visa to attend SA Peace Conference

43

A 'political settlement' is predicted as the National Prosecuting Authority
holds talks on whether to proceed with Zuma's corruption case

2 April 2009

Charges dropped, smells political. NPA chief Mokotedi Mpshe and deputy Willie Hofmeyr insist it's strictly legal: 'intolerable abuse' of process. A 2007 tape has surfaced on which former Scorpions boss Leonard McCarthy is heard trying to manipulate the timing of charges against Zuma.

8 April 2009

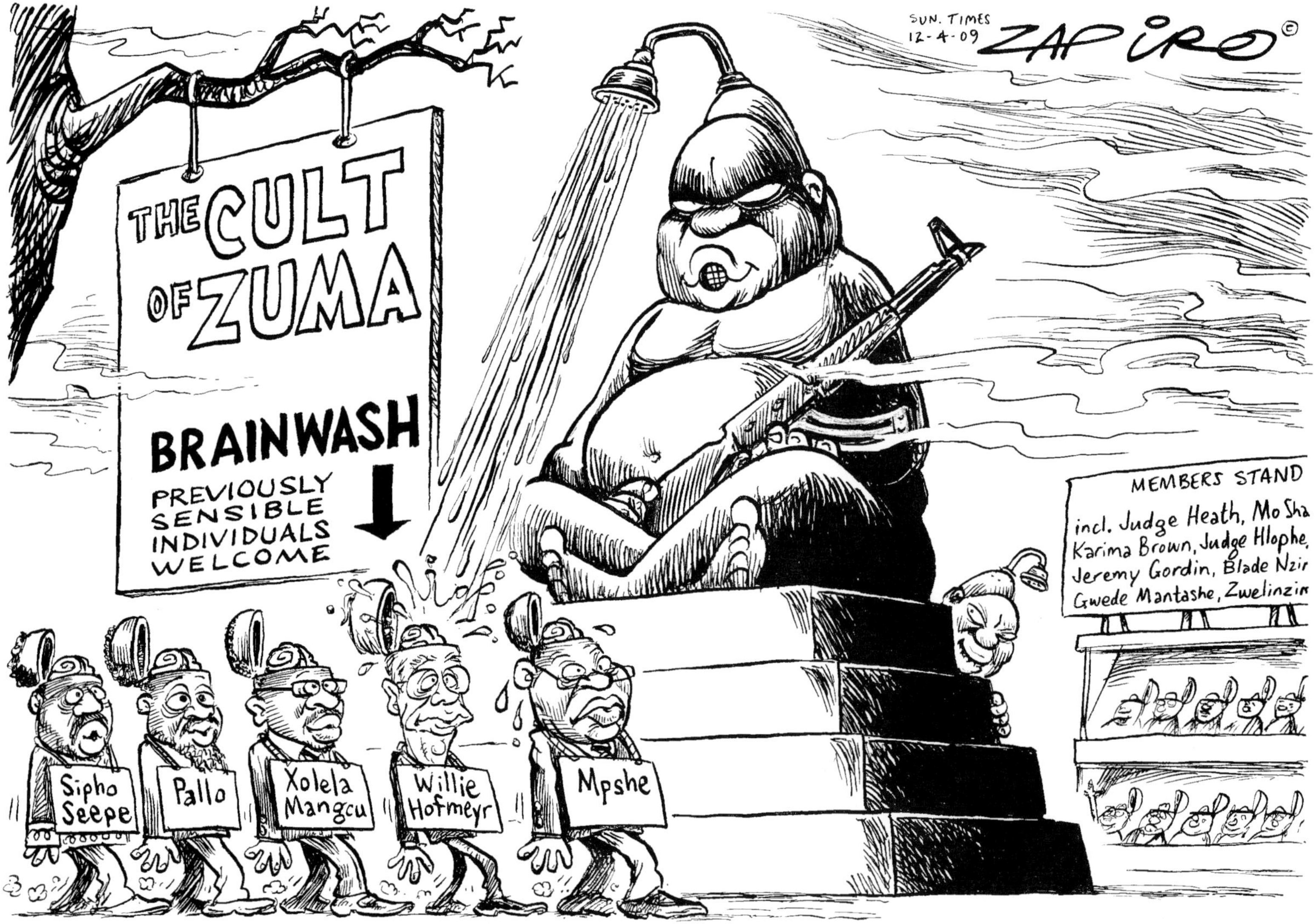
SUN. TIMES
12-4-09
ZAPIRO ©
THE CULT OF ZUMA
BRAINWASH
PREVIOUSLY SENSIBLE INDIVIDUALS WELCOME
MEMBERS STAND
incl. Judge Heath, Mo Sha
Karima Brown, Judge Hlophe,
Jeremy Gordin, Blade Nzir
Gwede Mantashe, Zwelinzin
Sipho Seepe
Pallo
Xolela Mangcu
Willie Hofmeyr
Mpshe

12 April 2009

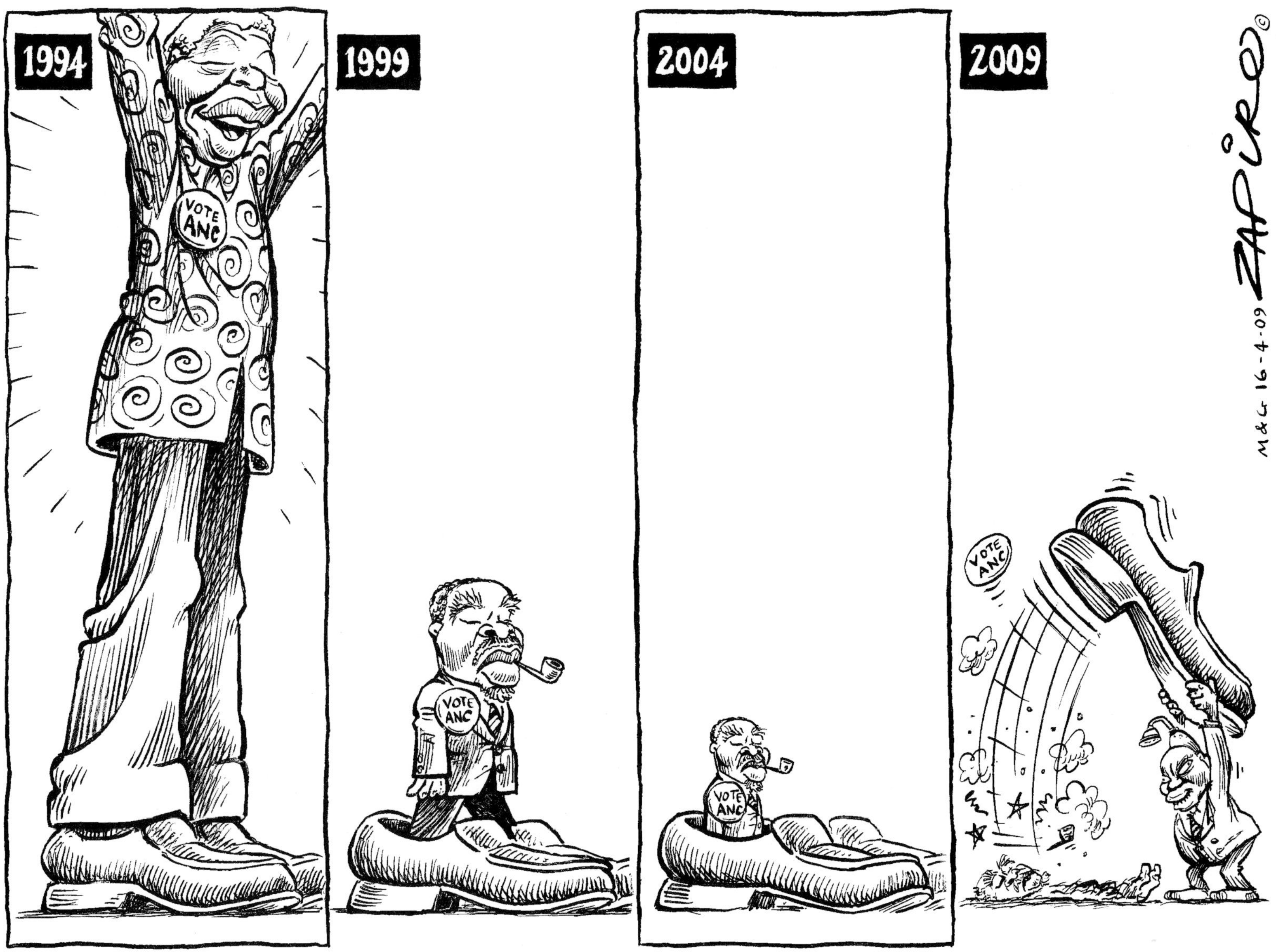
1994
VOTE ANC
1999
VOTE ANC
2004
VOTE ANC
2009
VOTE ANC
ZAPIRO
M&G 16-4-09

16 April 2009

Fourth democratic election

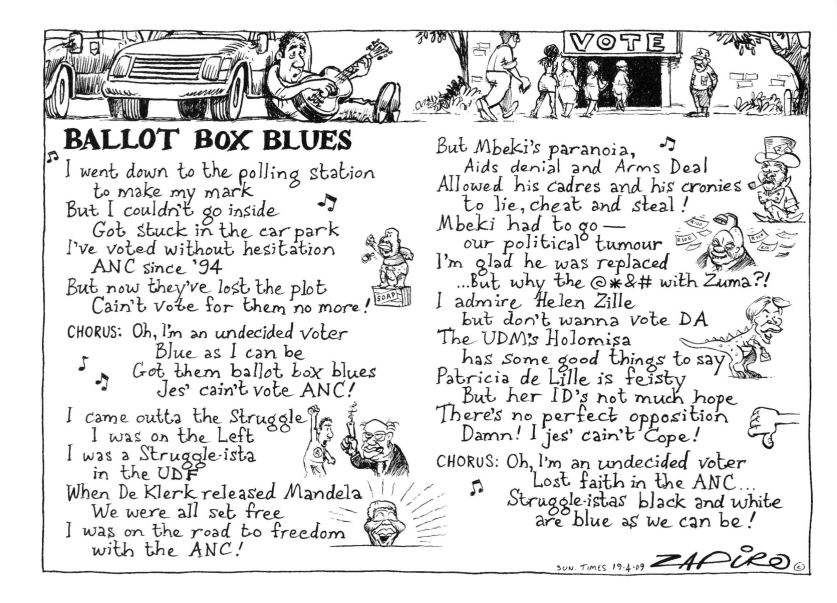

BALLOT BOX BLUES

I went down to the polling station
    to make my mark
But I couldn't go inside
    Got stuck in the car park
I've voted without hesitation
    ANC since '94
But now they've lost the plot
    Cain't vote for them no more!

CHORUS: Oh, I'm an undecided voter
    Blue as I can be
    Got them ballot box blues
    Jes' cain't vote ANC!

I came outta the Struggle
    I was on the Left
I was a Struggle-ista
    in the UDF
When De Klerk released Mandela
    We were all set free
I was on the road to freedom
    with the ANC!

But Mbeki's paranoia,
    Aids denial and Arms Deal
Allowed his cadres and his cronies
    to lie, cheat and steal!
Mbeki had to go —
    our political tumour
I'm glad he was replaced
    ...But why the @*&# with Zuma?!
I admire Helen Zille
    but don't wanna vote DA
The UDM's Holomisa
    has some good things to say
Patricia de Lille is feisty
    But her ID's not much hope
There's no perfect opposition
    Damn! I jes' cain't Cope!

CHORUS: Oh, I'm an undecided voter
    Lost faith in the ANC...
    Struggle-istas black and white
    are blue as we can be!

SUN. TIMES 19·4·09 ZAPIRO

19 April 2009

VOTE

PROMISES

M&G 23-4-09

ZAPIRO

23 April 2009

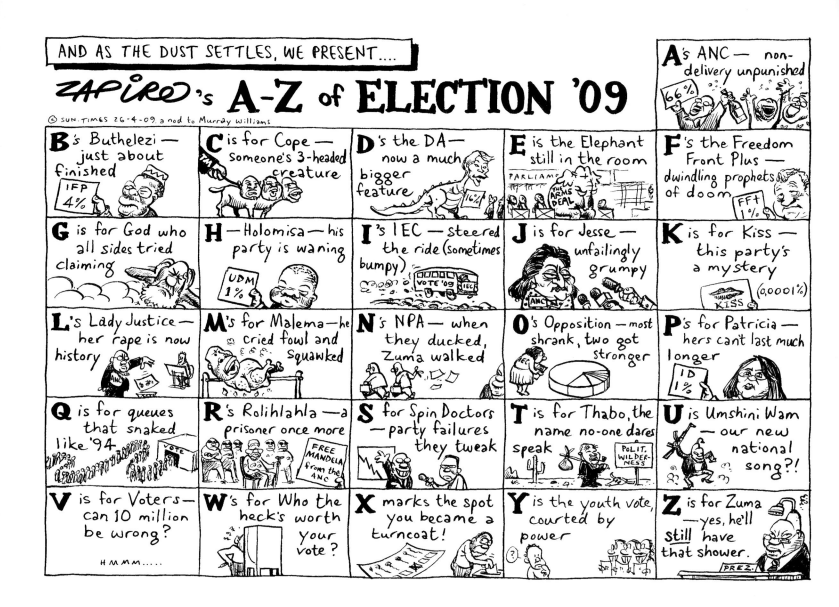

AND AS THE DUST SETTLES, WE PRESENT....

ZAPIRO's **A-Z** of **ELECTION '09**

© SUN-TIMES 26-4-09, a nod to Murray Williams

A's ANC — non-delivery unpunished 66%

B's Buthelezi — just about finished IFP 4%

C is for Cope — Someone's 3-headed creature

D's the DA — now a much bigger feature 16%

E is the Elephant still in the room PARLIAMENT THE ARMS DEAL

F's the Freedom Front Plus — dwindling prophets of doom FF+ 1%

G is for God who all sides tried claiming

H — Holomisa — his party is waning UDM 1%

I's IEC — steered the ride (sometimes bumpy) VOTE '09 IEC

J is for Jesse — unfailingly grumpy ANC

K is for Kiss — this party's a mystery KISS (0,0001%)

L's Lady Justice — her rape is now history ANC

M's for Malema — he cried fowl and squawked

N's NPA — when they ducked, Zuma walked

O's Opposition — most shrank, two got stronger

P's for Patricia — hers can't last much longer ID 1%

Q is for queues that snaked like '94 VOTE

R's Rolihlahla — a prisoner once more FREE MANDELA from the ANC

S for Spin Doctors — party failures they tweak

T is for Thabo, the name no-one dares speak POLIT. WILDER-NESS

U is Umshini Wam — our new national song?!

V is for Voters — can 10 million be wrong? HMMM.....

W's for Who the heck's worth your vote?

X marks the spot you became a turncoat!

Y is the youth vote, courted by power ?

Z is for Zuma — yes, he'll _still_ have that shower. PREZ.

26 April 2009

50

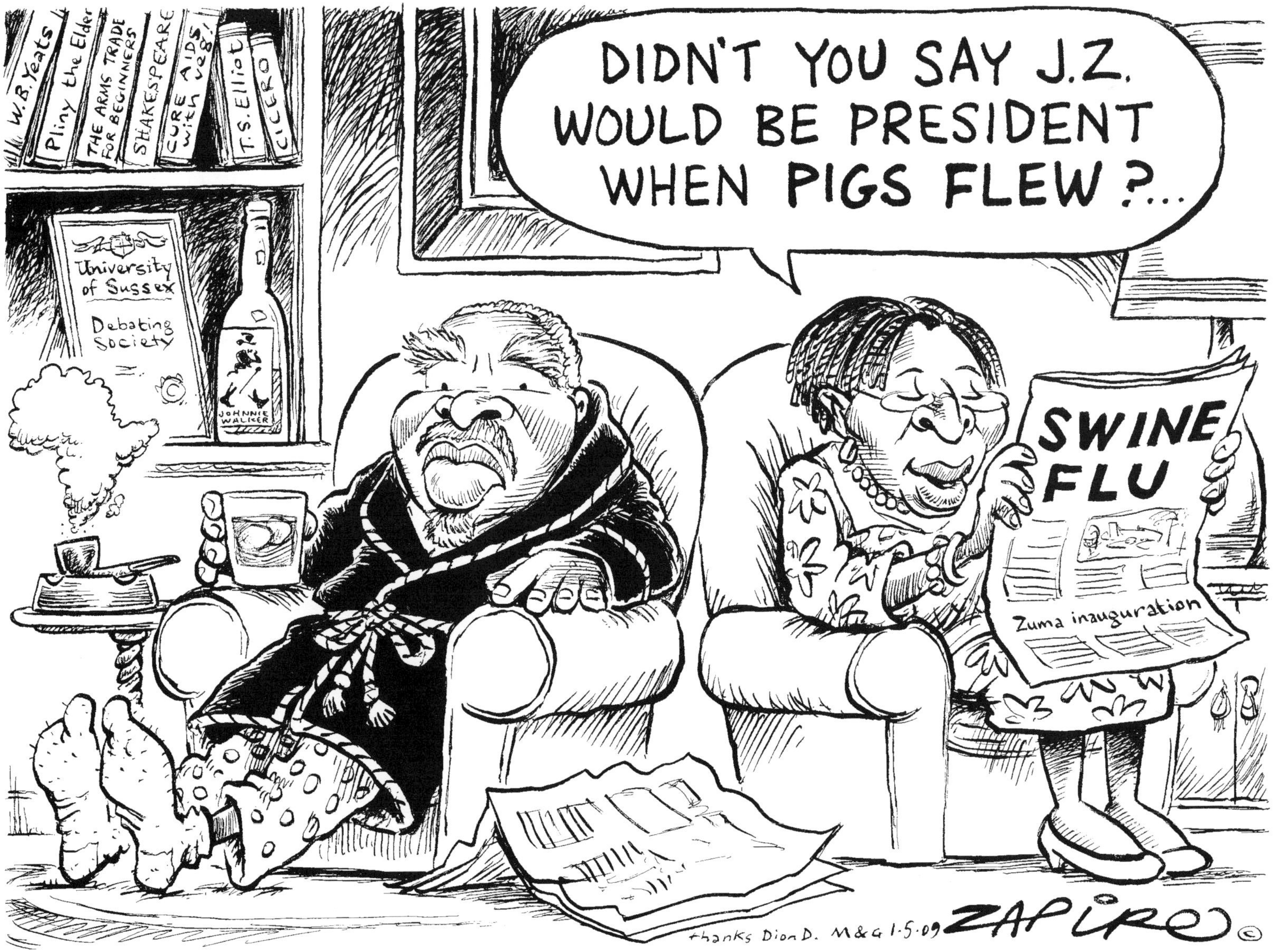
DIDN'T YOU SAY J.Z. WOULD BE PRESIDENT WHEN PIGS FLEW ?...
W.B.Yeats
Pliny the Elder
THE ARMS TRADE FOR BEGINNERS
SHAKESPEARE
CURE AIDS with veg!
T.S. Elliot
CICERO
University of Sussex
Debating Society
JOHNNIE WALKER
SWINE FLU
Zuma inauguration
thanks Dion D. M&G 1·5·09
ZAPIRO ©

1 May 2009

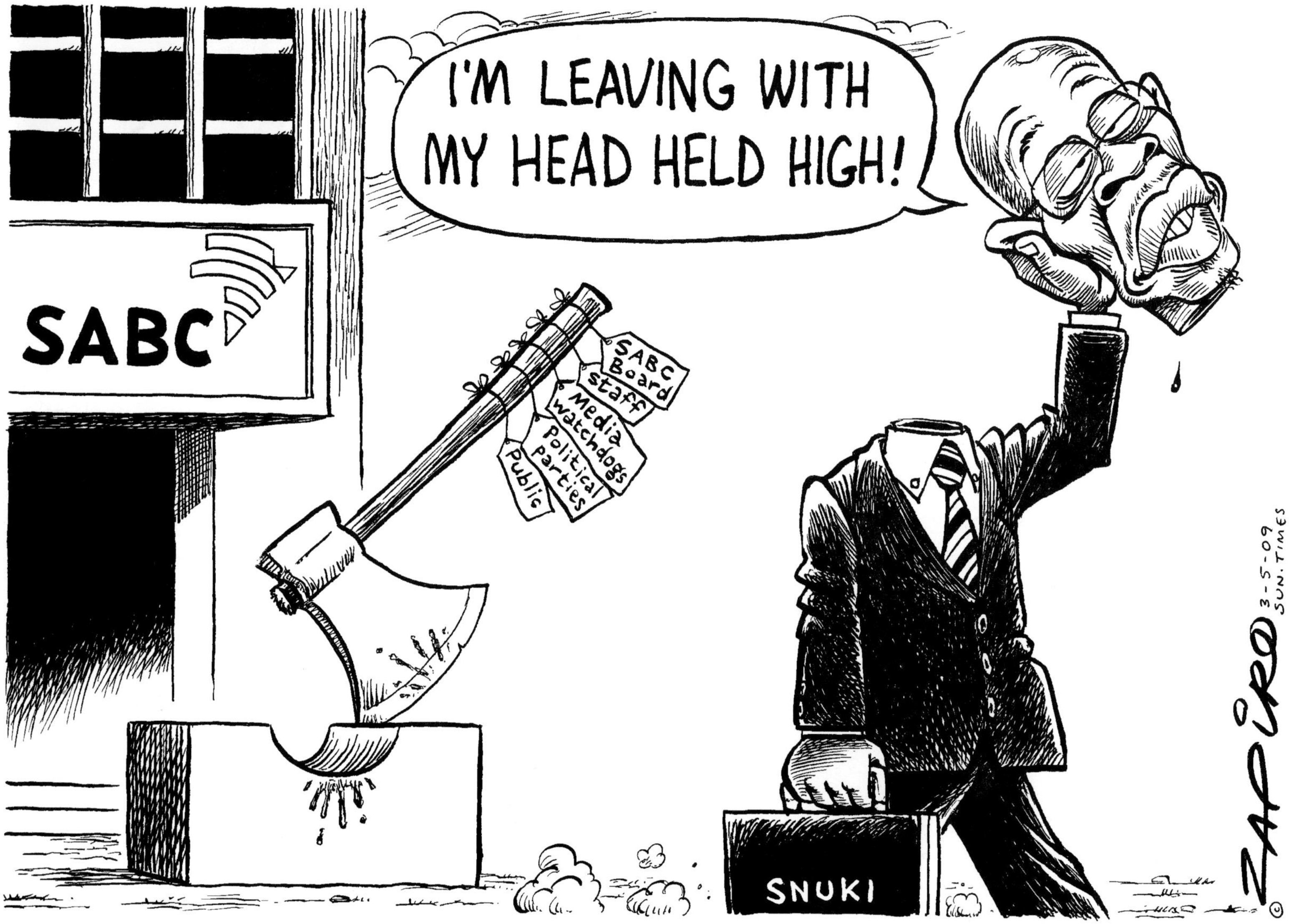
I'M LEAVING WITH MY HEAD HELD HIGH!
SABC
SABC Board
staff
Media watchdogs
Political parties
Public
SNUKI
ZAPIRO
3-5-09 SUN.TIMES
©

3 May 2009

Direct quote from the man who blacklisted critical commentators.
Head of news Snuki Zikalala's contract won't be renewed.

7 May 2009

Ahead of the big day (on which, funnily enough, it rained)

FIRST ITEM OF BUSINESS:

HOW TO REMOVE SHOWERHEAD

1. Hacksaw (tough)
2. File (tougher)
3. Sledgehammer (don't miss)
4. Blowtorch (ouch)
5. Chainsaw (scary)
6. Or try being truly presidential and maybe it'll just fall off.

ZAPIRO SUN. TIMES 10-5-09

10 May 2009

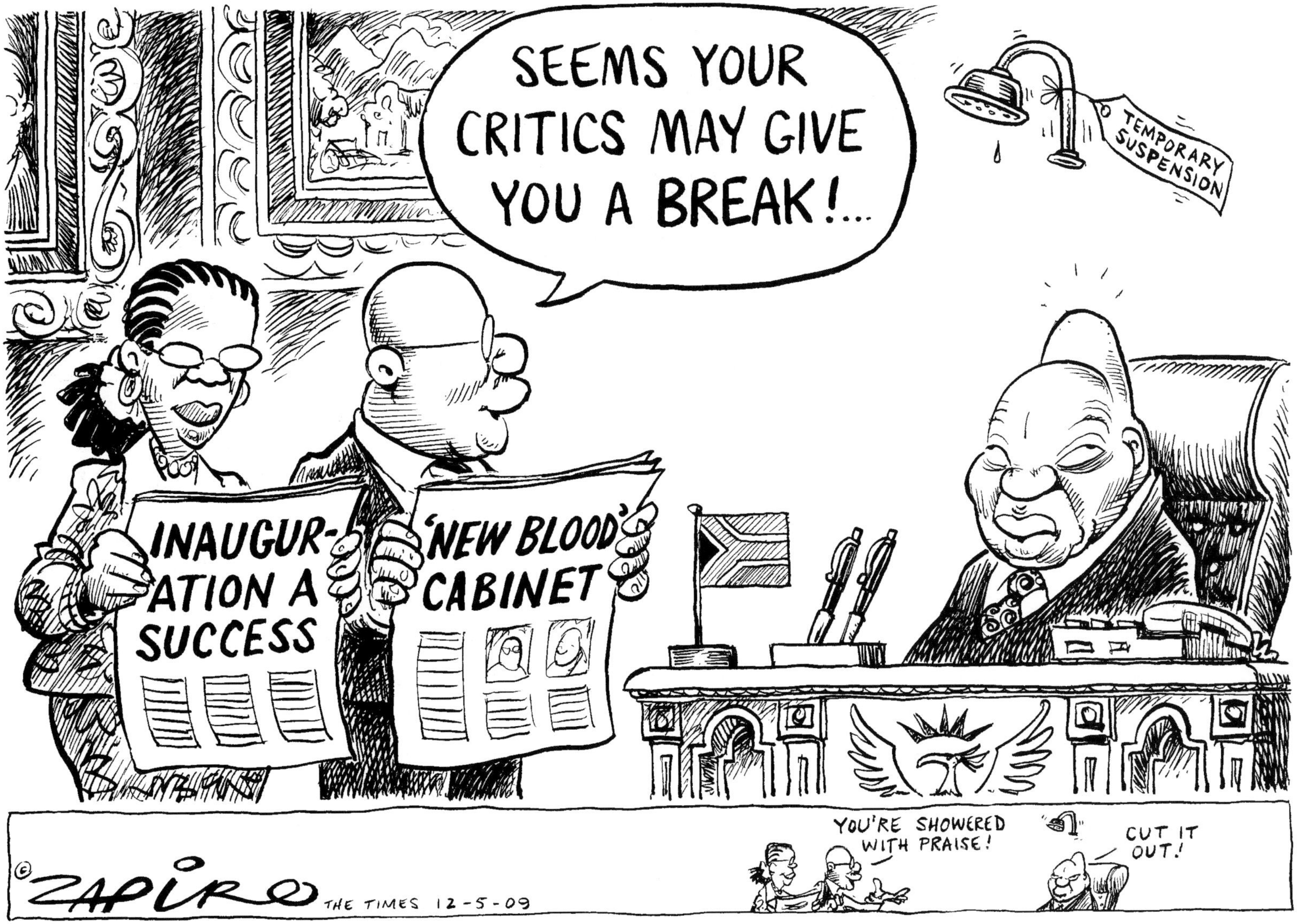
SEEMS YOUR CRITICS MAY GIVE YOU A BREAK!...
TEMPORARY SUSPENSION
INAUGUR-ATION A SUCCESS
'NEW BLOOD' CABINET
YOU'RE SHOWERED WITH PRAISE!
CUT IT OUT!
© ZAPIRO THE TIMES 12-5-09

12 May 2009

Deflecting ANC criticism of her all-male cabinet, Cape premier Helen Zille calls Zuma a womanising HIV-risk to his wives. The ANC's Youth League and military veterans say Zille's cabinet men are her 'concubines' – 'sex boys to satisfy her well-evolved wild-whore libido'.

14 May 2009

17 May 2009   ANC distances itself from Youth League diatribe

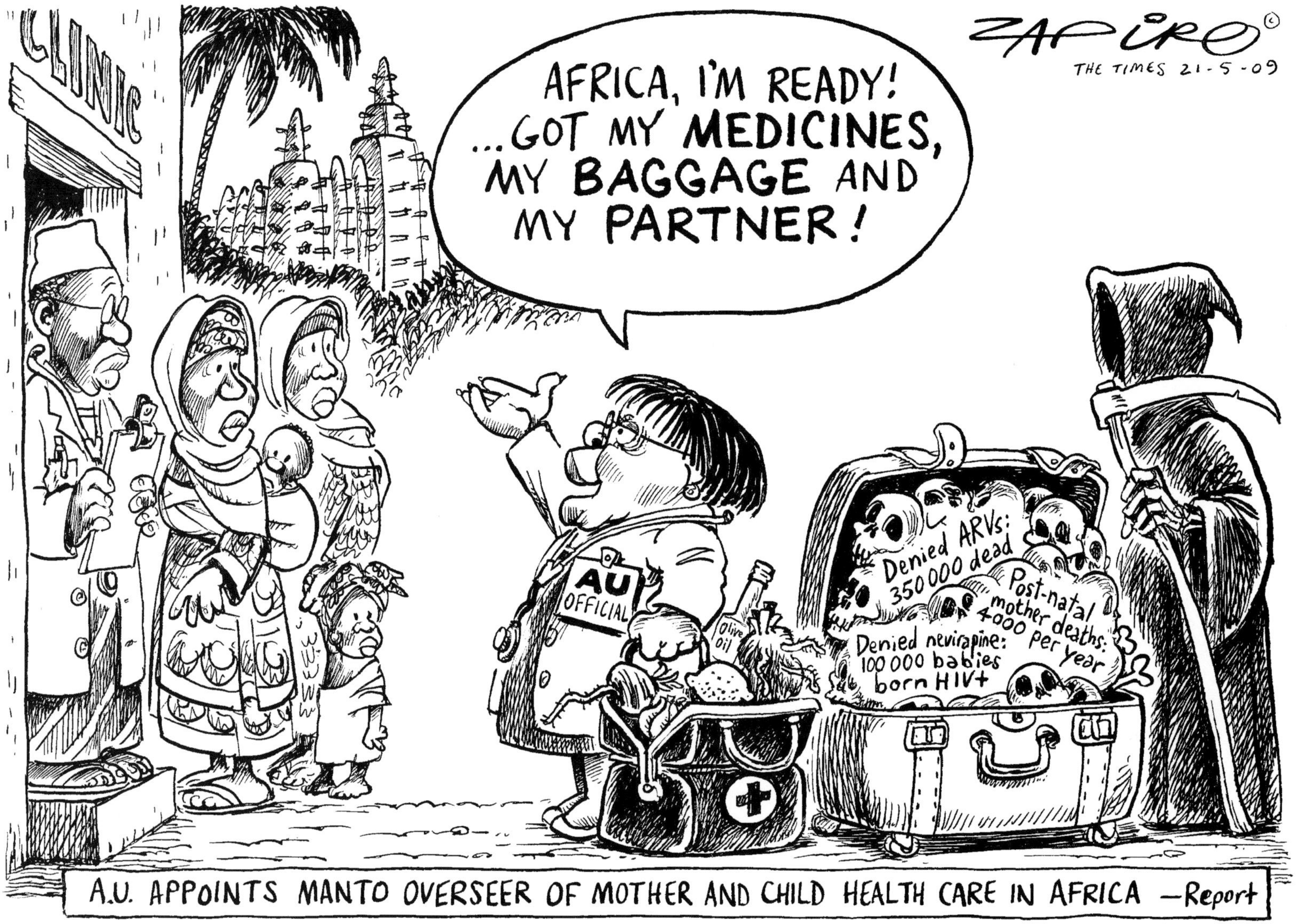
ZAPIRO ©
THE TIMES 21-5-09
CLINIC
AFRICA, I'M READY! ...GOT MY MEDICINES, MY BAGGAGE AND MY PARTNER!
AU OFFICIAL
Olive oil
Denied ARVs: 350 000 dead
Post-natal mother deaths: 4000 per year
Denied nevirapine: 100 000 babies born HIV+
A.U. APPOINTS MANTO OVERSEER OF MOTHER AND CHILD HEALTH CARE IN AFRICA —Report

21 May 2009

19 May 2009

New minister receives a R1,1 million Merc and two cows from grateful contractors whom he'd previously awarded R10 billion of transport contracts. He sees no conflict of interest.

After media outcry he consults his boss, but in the end
wisely ignores the strange advice to simply declare the gift

21 May 2009

60

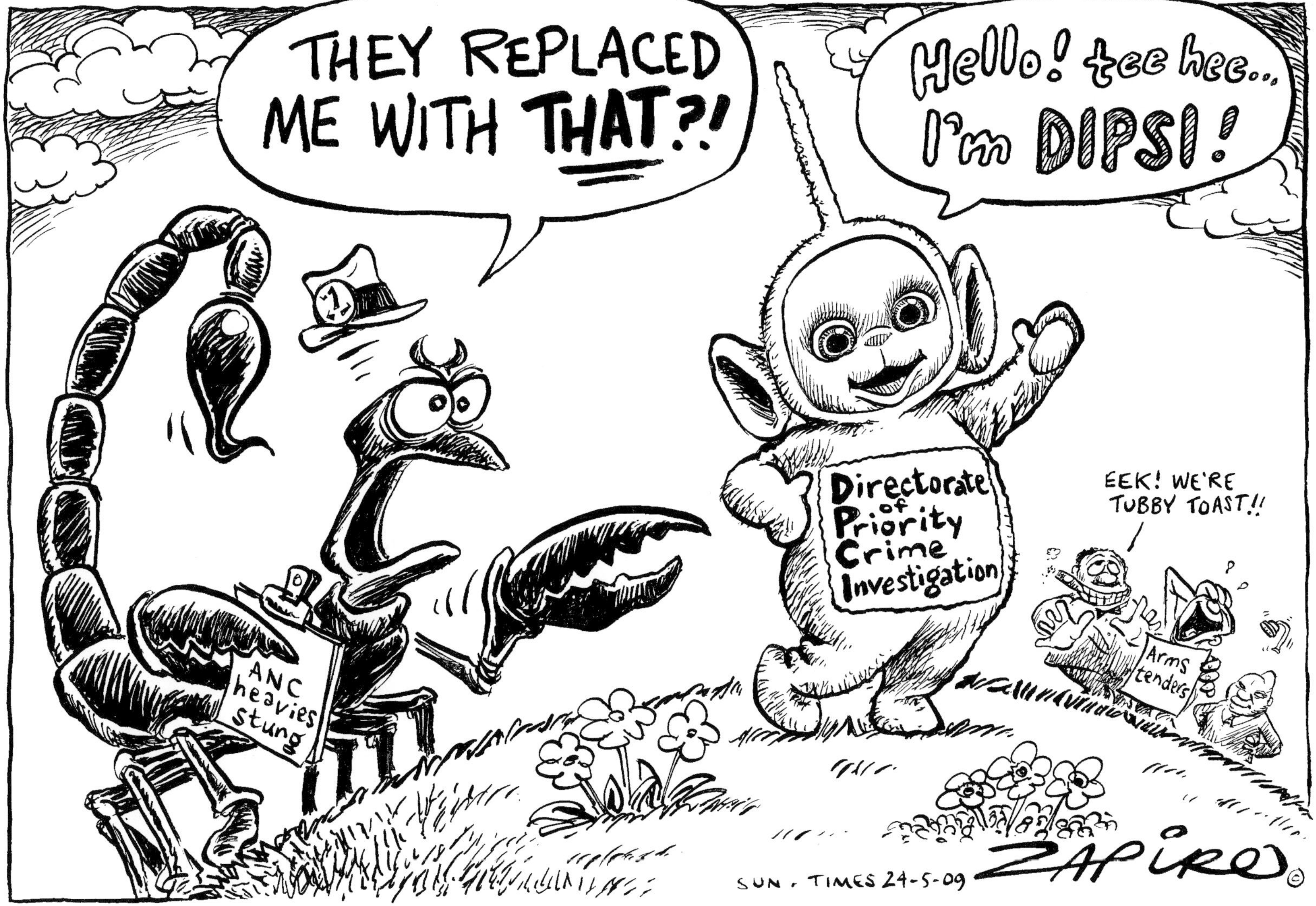
THEY REPLACED ME WITH THAT?!
Hello! tee hee... I'm DIPSI!
ANC heavies stung
Directorate of Priority Crime Investigation
EEK! WE'RE TUBBY TOAST!!
Arms tenders
SUN - TIMES 24-5-09
ZAPIRO ©

24 May 2009

New unit named

26 May 2009

Ambitious Cape Judge President John Hlophe, facing a Judicial Service Commission hearing for trying to influence Constitutional Court judges to favour Zuma, tries to scupper the hearing by accusing then-justice minister Enver Surtee of having a political agenda

" ...the programme on political satire will not be aired because due process with regards to consultation has not been concluded. "

SABC

ZAPIRO 28-5-09 THE TIMES

A pre-election Special Assignment documentary on SA satire (featuring the 'Rape of Justice' cartoon for which the president is suing me) was cancelled by the SABC. Weeks later they advertise it again, only to cancel again at the last minute.

28 May 2009

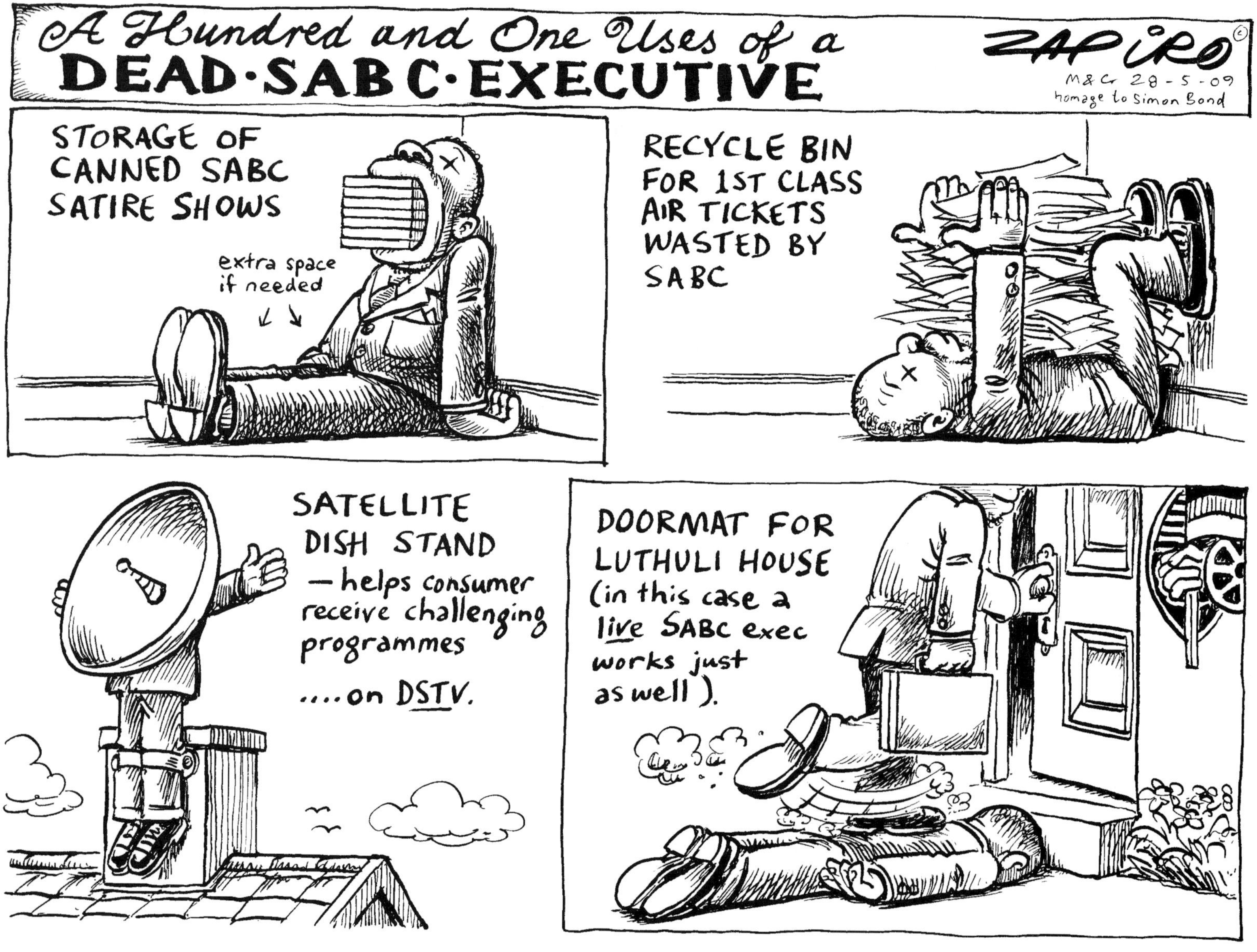
A Hundred and One Uses of a
DEAD·SABC·EXECUTIVE
ZAPIRO©
M&G 28-5-09
homage to Simon Bond
STORAGE OF CANNED SABC SATIRE SHOWS
extra space if needed
RECYCLE BIN FOR 1ST CLASS AIR TICKETS WASTED BY SABC
SATELLITE DISH STAND
—helps consumer receive challenging programmes
....on DSTV.
DOORMAT FOR LUTHULI HOUSE
(in this case a live SABC exec works just as well).

28 May 2009

WHICH NORTH KOREAN NUCLEAR WARHEAD SHOULD CONCERN US MOST?

SHORT RANGE

LONG RANGE

DERANGED

ZAPIRO SUN.TIMES 31-5-09

Claiming a capability of striking as far as the US, Kim Jong Il's army detonates
a nuclear missile and threatens war if Korea-bound ships are searched for nukes

2 June 2009

44 false killer whales put down when they beach themselves at Kommetjie. There've been threats to make the province ungovernable after mutual mud-slinging over Zille's all-male mostly white cabinet.

3 June 2009

The new administration that's promised to increase
social spending and create jobs is rattled by a 6,4% drop in GDP

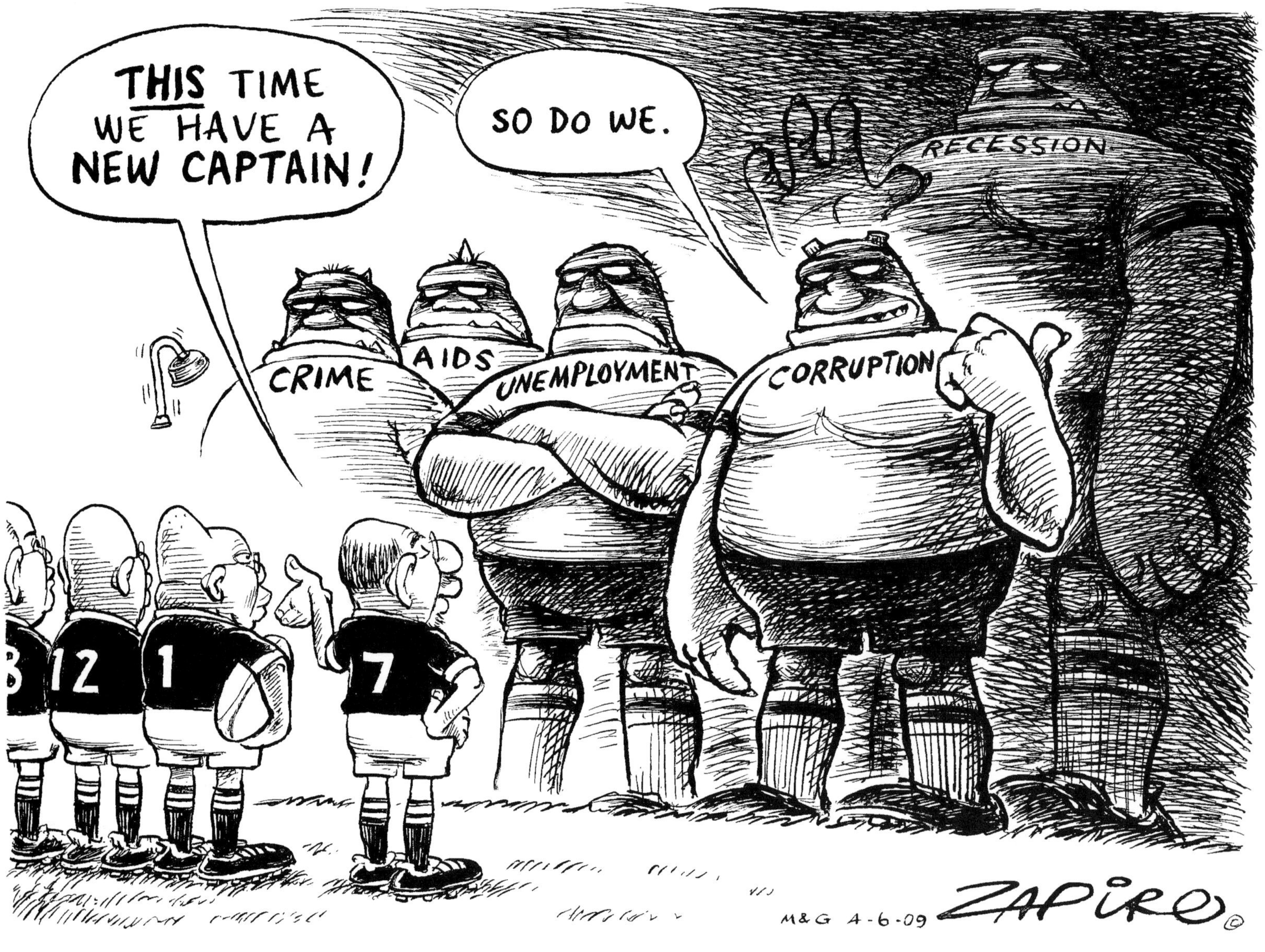
THIS TIME WE HAVE A NEW CAPTAIN!
SO DO WE.
CRIME
AIDS
UNEMPLOYMENT
CORRUPTION
RECESSION
8
12
1
7
M&G 4-6-09
ZAPIRO ©

4 June 2009

TIANANMEN SQUARE: A MOMENT OF SILENCE FOR THE VICTIMS

7-6-09
SUN.TIMES ZAPIRO©

7 June 2009

Twenty years since the Tiananmen Square Massacre. Clampdown again by Chinese authorities against images and info about the thousands of protesting students killed when tanks rolled into Beijing.

69

THE TIMES
9-6-09
ZAPIRO

9 June 2009

Obama's speech in Cairo appealing to the Muslim and Arab
world for a new beginning in their relationship with the United States

11 June 2009

Occasion marked by much publicity … and by our non-performing team's
R35 million demand in the unlikely event they win the upcoming Confederations Cup

11 June 2009   Cape Town hosts the World Economic Forum on Africa

14 June 2009

Aiding transformation or installing compliant judges? Jeff Radebe gets the Judicial Service Commission to delay new judicial appointments until after the JSC itself gets new politically-appointed members.

16 June 2009

ANC Secretary-General Gwede Mantashe has recently summoned a cabinet minister
to party HQ Luthuli House where he's also held meetings to sort out government issues

74

21 June 2009   New party in disarray: factionalism, confusion over leadership, defections back to the ANC

18 June 2009

The mess at the SABC is widely blamed on the board installed by Mbeki.
Now most board members resign and ANC MPs pressure the rest to do so too.

SABC BORED

24 June 2009

Internal squabbles, industrial strikes and new programmes
drying up as the board's being dissolved by parliament

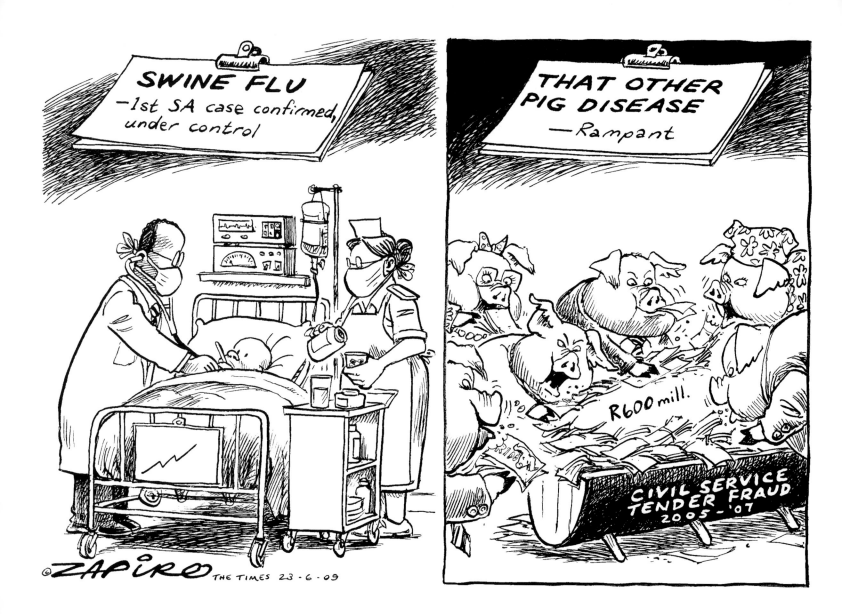

23 June 2009

Auditor-general's probe finds 2 000 officials awarded tenders
to companies owned by themselves, their spouses or their relatives

25 June 2009

After President Ahmadinejad's dodgy re-election, he and Supreme
Leader Khatami can't hide the bloody clampdown on protesting students

28 June 2009   Dying aged 50 of cardiac arrest probably caused by injected painkiller

30 June 2009

Despite some transport problems, we've paved the way for next year by hosting a highly successful Confederations Cup tournament. Even Bafana Bafana played better than usual.

HOLLOW VICTORY

LIONS

2 July 2009

Trademark wacky soundbytes from coach Peter de Villiers after Boks beat
touring Brits, only this time he condones eye-gouging by flanker Schalk Burger

2 July 2009

As the King of Pop is buried

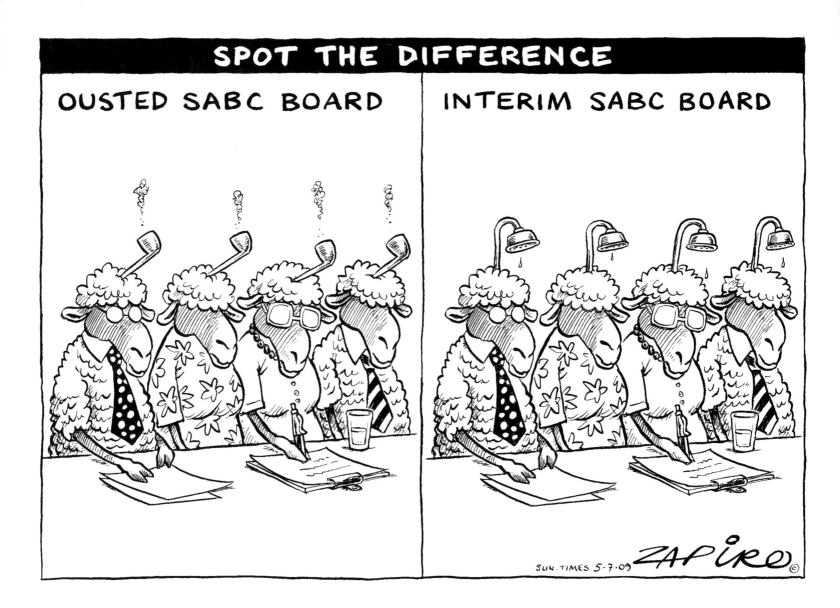

5 July 2009

ANC candidates bulldozed in yet again

7 July 2009

Dockets hidden or burned, senior officers implicated

9 July 2009

Snappy title for the elite unit replacing the Scorpions

PARTY LEADERS DRAW INSPIRATION FROM THEIR MENTOR

9 July 2009

Playing down leadership battles, unpaid bills and resignation of
party deputy president Lynda Odendaal and elections head Simon Grindrod

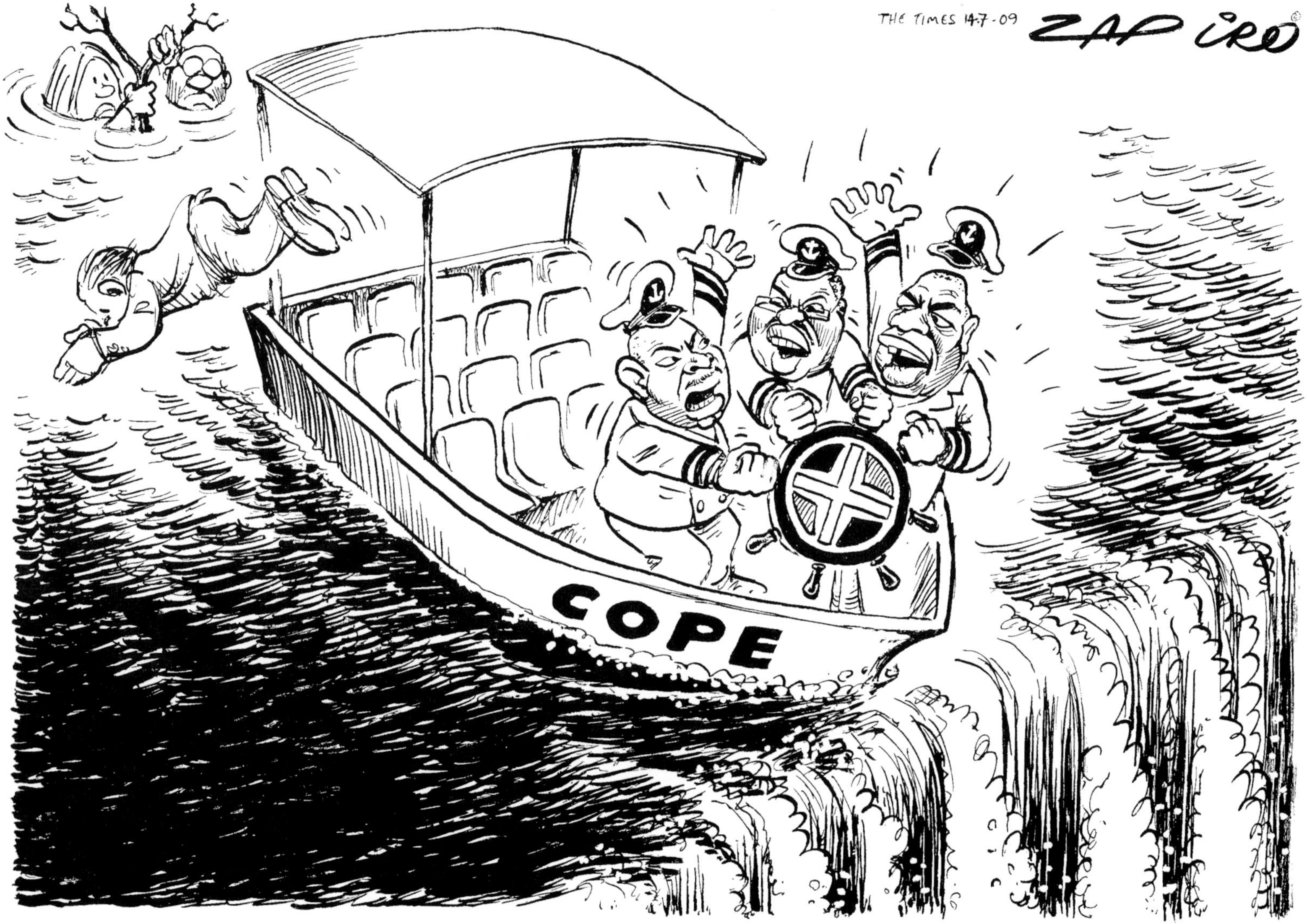
THE TIMES 14-7-09
ZAPIRO
COPE

14 July 2009

12 July 2009

'Those who had a nice time will ask for breakfast and taxi money.' – the comment about Zuma's rape accuser that lands him in the Equality Court, and he's not sorry

16 July 2009

Former Liberian president on trial for 500 000 murders
and mutilations in Sierra Leone's 1991–2002 civil war

16 July 2009

It's 40 years since the first manned lunar landing.
And it's the first global Mandela Day on his 91st birthday.

HIS 46664 CONCERTS: RAISED TENS OF MILLIONS FOR AIDS

HIS CHILDREN'S FUND: RAISED HUNDREDS OF MILLIONS FOR KIDS

WHAT HE INSPIRES IN US: PRICELESS.

19-7-09 SUN.TIMES ZAPIRO

19 July 2009   '64 Minutes for Mandela': people everywhere serve humanity as he has done for 64 years

THE TIMES 21-7-09   ZAPIRO

21 July 2009

But his grandson Mandla uses the occasion to claim the icon's legacy for the family
and the ANC, echoing Zuma's pre-election rebuff of the Nelson Mandela Foundation

23 July 2009   Nationwide eruption of protests, many of them violent, against abysmal local government

Promising angry marchers a clean-out of lazy councillors
and an assurance that his administration really will be different

26 July 2009

28 July 2009   Now there are strikes as well. Oh yes, and a series of ANC Siyabonga (thank you) rallies.

30 July 2009

Growing trend in civil service strikes all over

The JSC, now bolstered with Zuma appointees, is set to flout a high court ruling that the hearing into Judge Hlophe's conduct must be held in public

30 July 2009

98

2 August 2009

Overlooking police professionals, Zuma picks his old
political ally Bheki Cele as new National Police Commissioner

Starting out with a call for a moratorium on crime stats

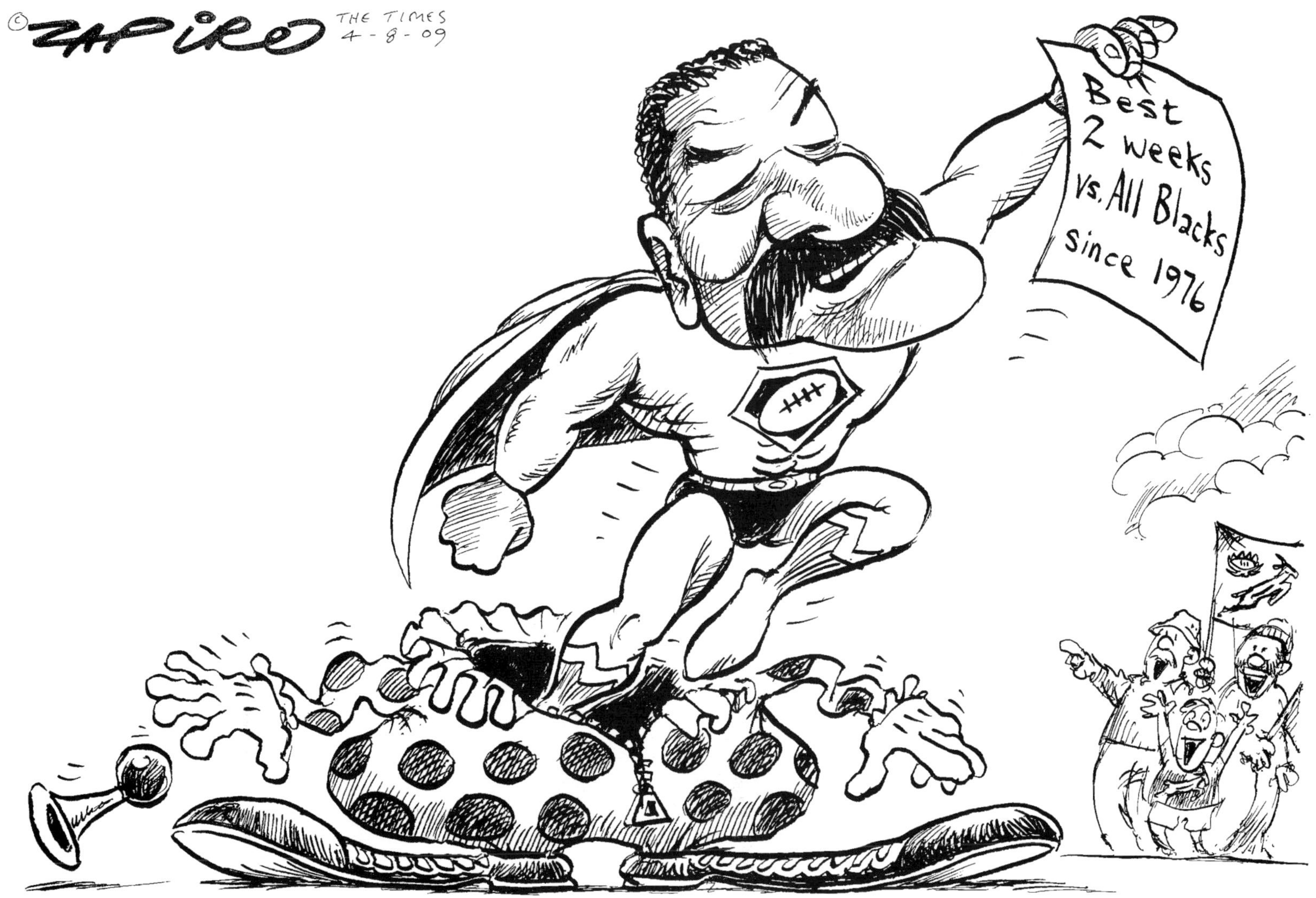
©ZAPIRO THE TIMES 4-8-09
Best 2 weeks vs. All Blacks since 1976

4 August 2009

6 August 2009

Surprise visit catches mayor at home in working hours

9 August 2009

US Secretary of State Hillary Clinton's impressive
African tour and her husband's retrieval of two jailed Americans

13 August 2009   Unable to refute his damaging claims, they're trying to nail him for disclosing classified info

13 August 2009

He thought he was off the record when he sparked his latest furore, this time
with racial remarks about Chief Justice Pius Langa to whom he now writes to explain

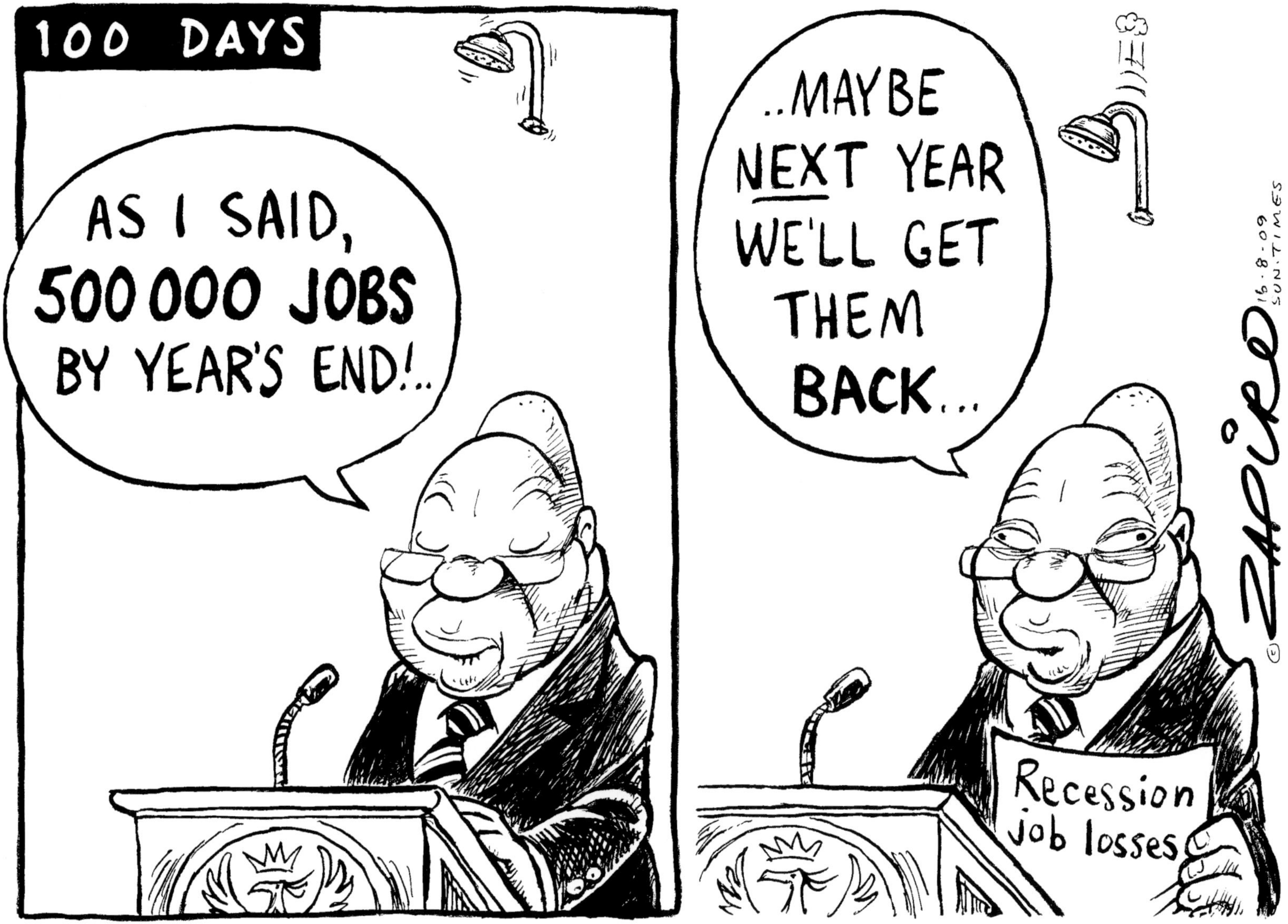
100 DAYS
AS I SAID, 500 000 JOBS BY YEAR'S END!..
..MAYBE NEXT YEAR WE'LL GET THEM BACK...
Recession job losses
16·8·09 SUN·TIMES

16 August 2009

20 August 2009

High marks for his affable and inclusive approach

18 August 2009

His record is dismal, but former SABC CEO Dali Mpofu gets a
huge payout in return for dropping his legal challenge to his suspension

Usain Bolt shredded sprint records at last year's
Olympics and does so again at Berlin's World Championships

23 August 2009

SA teenager Caster Semenya smashes the field to win 800m gold, shrugging off the pre-race announcement that the International Association of Athletics Federations is to test her gender

110

IAAF rightly slated, though Malema and others cry racism on flimsy grounds.
It's also emerging that Athletics SA headed by Leonard Chuene has let Caster down.

25 August 2009

27 August 2009

Huge welcome overshadowed by the Julius/Winnie/Chuene show blaming Europeans and hostile local media

27 August 2009

Leaked government report links Deputy President Motlanthe to kickbacks
paid in 2004 to Saddam's regime to secure Iraqi oil deals benefiting the ANC

At the Union Buildings, protesting soldiers wielding handmade weapons
and petrol bombs clash with police who fire rubber bullets and stun grenades

AS SEEN BY JO'BURG'S TAXI DRIVERS

1 September 2009

Long-awaited Bus Rapid Transit system launched.
Taxi operators facing a loss of income threaten violence.

3 September 2009   Ruling that Brandon Huntley's 'fear of persecution by African South Africans' is justified

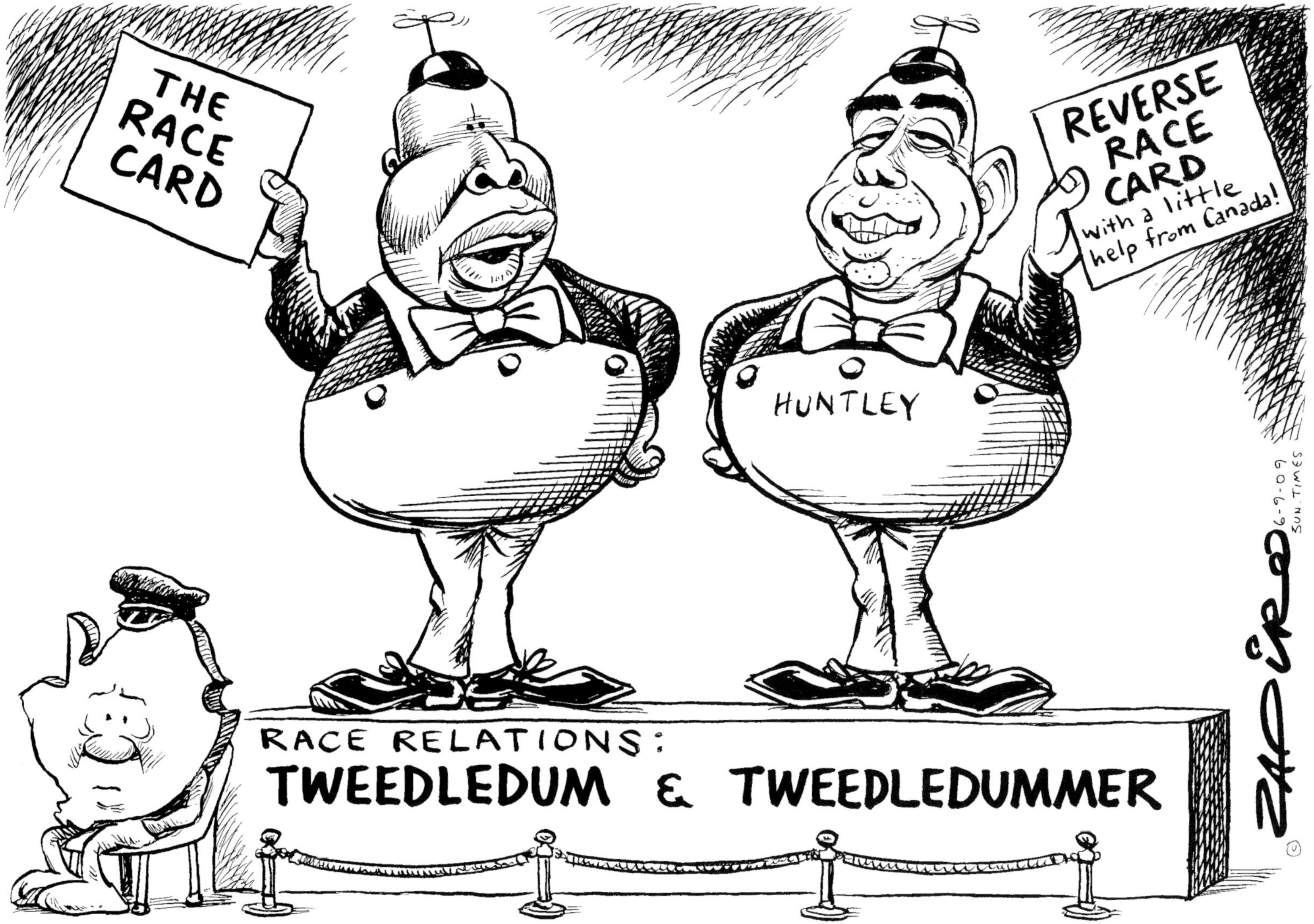
THE RACE CARD
REVERSE RACE CARD with a little help from Canada!
HUNTLEY
RACE RELATIONS:
TWEEDLEDUM & TWEEDLEDUMMER
6-9-09 SUN. TIMES

6 September 2009

3 September 2009

Divided JSC decides there'll be no misconduct
probe into Hlophe's whisperings to Concourt judges

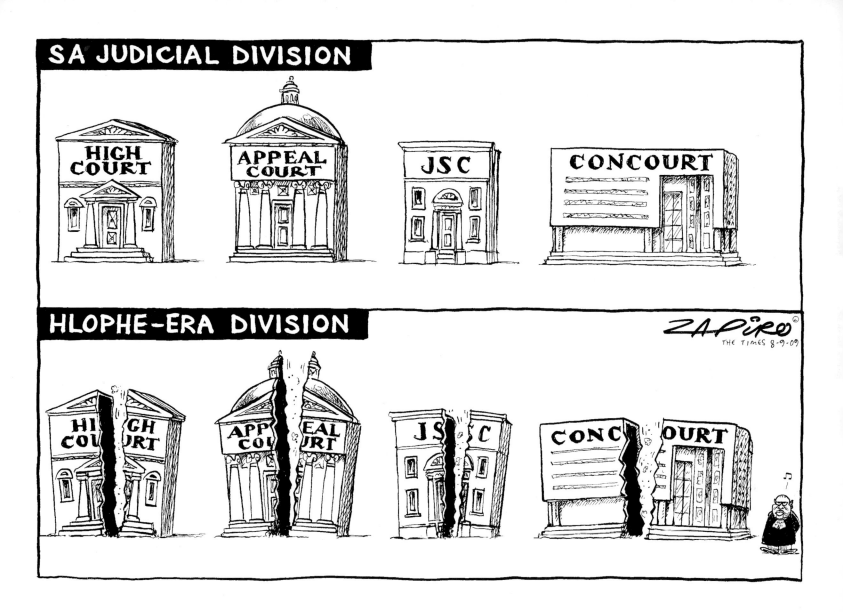

No end to the saga: former Concourt judge Johann Kriegler
mounts a legal challenge against the JSC cop-out

8 September 2009

Cosatu wants Higher Education Minister Blade Nzimande
and other cabinet big spenders to return their cars

10 September 2009

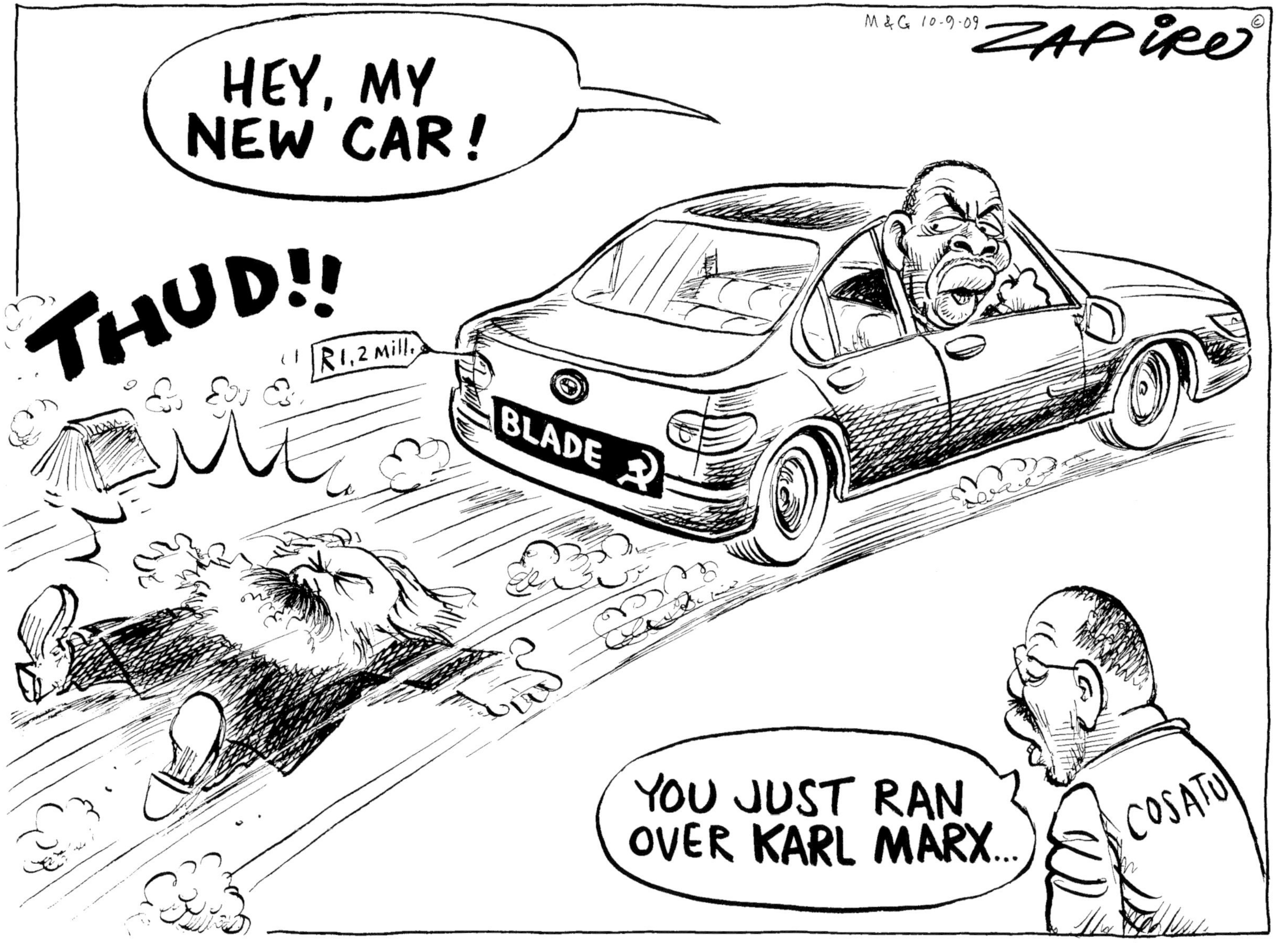
M&G 10·9·09 ZAPIRO ©
HEY, MY NEW CAR!
THUD!!
R1,2 Mill.
BLADE
YOU JUST RAN OVER KARL MARX...
COSATU

10 September 2009

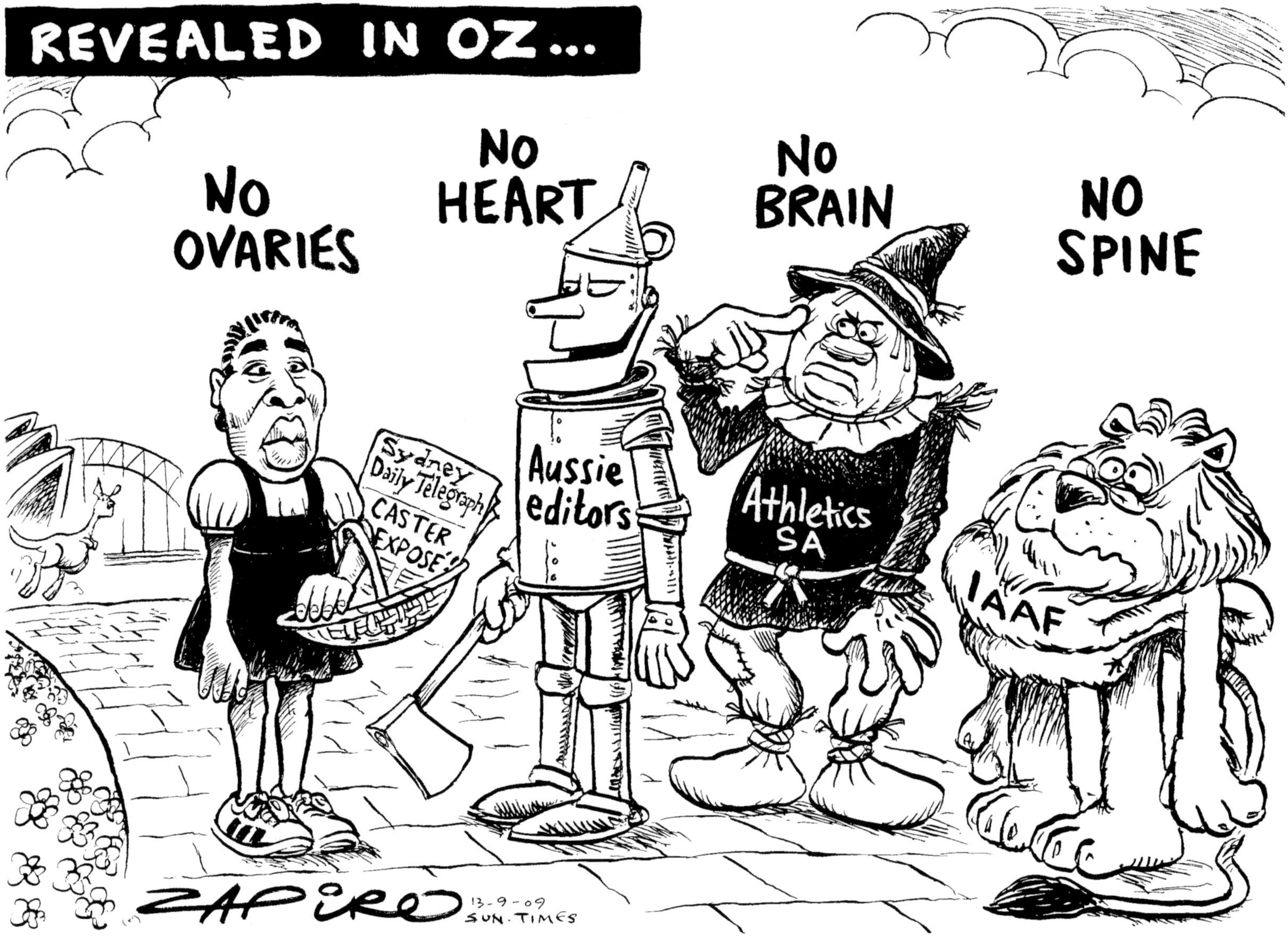
REVEALED IN OZ...
NO OVARIES
NO HEART
NO BRAIN
NO SPINE
Sydney Daily Telegraph
CASTER EXPOSÉ!
Aussie editors
Athletics SA
IAAF
ZAPIRO 13-9-09 SUN. TIMES

13 September 2009

Leaked medical report published

15 September 2009

80km test using data chip strapped to bird's leg

Taking co-responsibility for the failure of Outcomes Based Education

17 September 2009   Rhema Church head Ray McCauley's conservative coalition gains ground

Just a year after Mbeki's removal, rumours of a plot to oust Motlanthe
and Mantashe from the running and block a second term for Zuma.
And Julius Malema (!) is eyeing the presidency.

20 September 2009

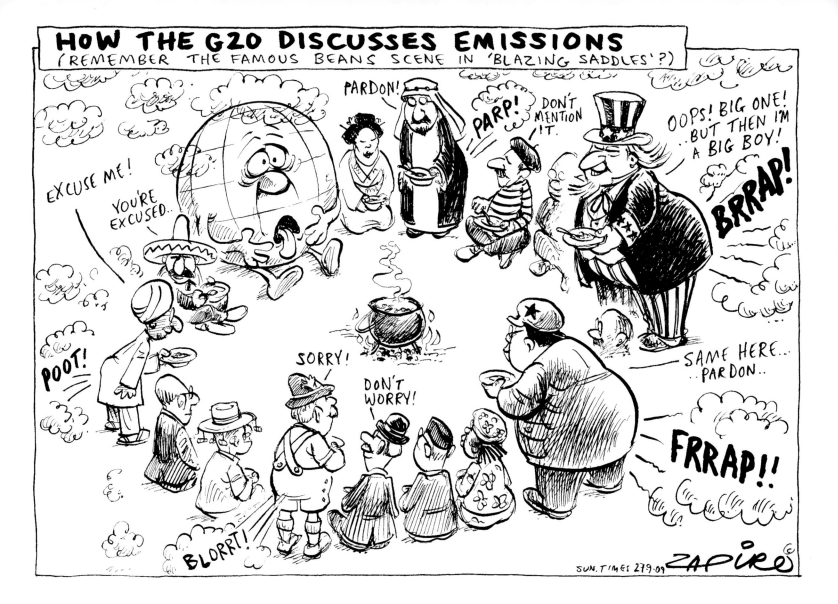

27 September 2009   In Pittsburgh, USA, negotiating climate finance based on 'national circumstances'

29 September 2009   SA trade mission during escalating tension over missile tests and a new plant

22 September 2009   Inflammatory talk while easing restrictions on police use of deadly force

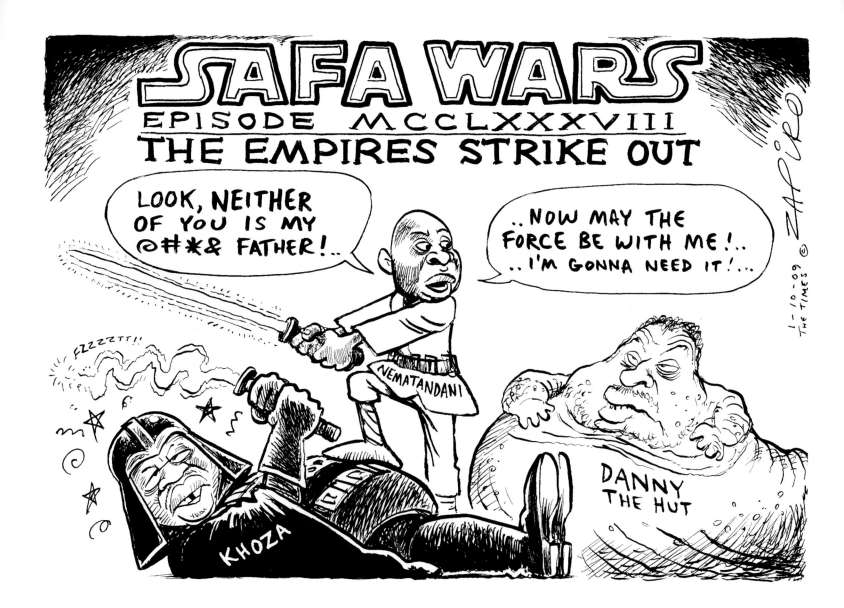

1 October 2009

When Danny Jordaan quits soccer's bitter presidential battle, his
campaigner Kirsten Nematandani surprises the powerful Irvin Khoza

4 October 2009

Informing us there's no word for hermaphrodite in Pedi, so
Caster Semenya's condition is an imperialist concept that doesn't exist

131

The National Intelligence Agency responds to the *Mail & Guardian's* complaint

INTELLIGENCE
HEAD

MOE

6 October 2009   Moe Shaik, that old Zuma ally with dubious family ties, is to head the SA Secret Service

8 October 2009

Famous proclamation of friendship recalled in the trial of former police chief Jackie Selebi
as convicted drug lord Glenn Agliotti testifies he had Selebi on his payroll for years

134

Selebi claims two former top prosecutors took bribes.
And there's a date error on the charge sheet.

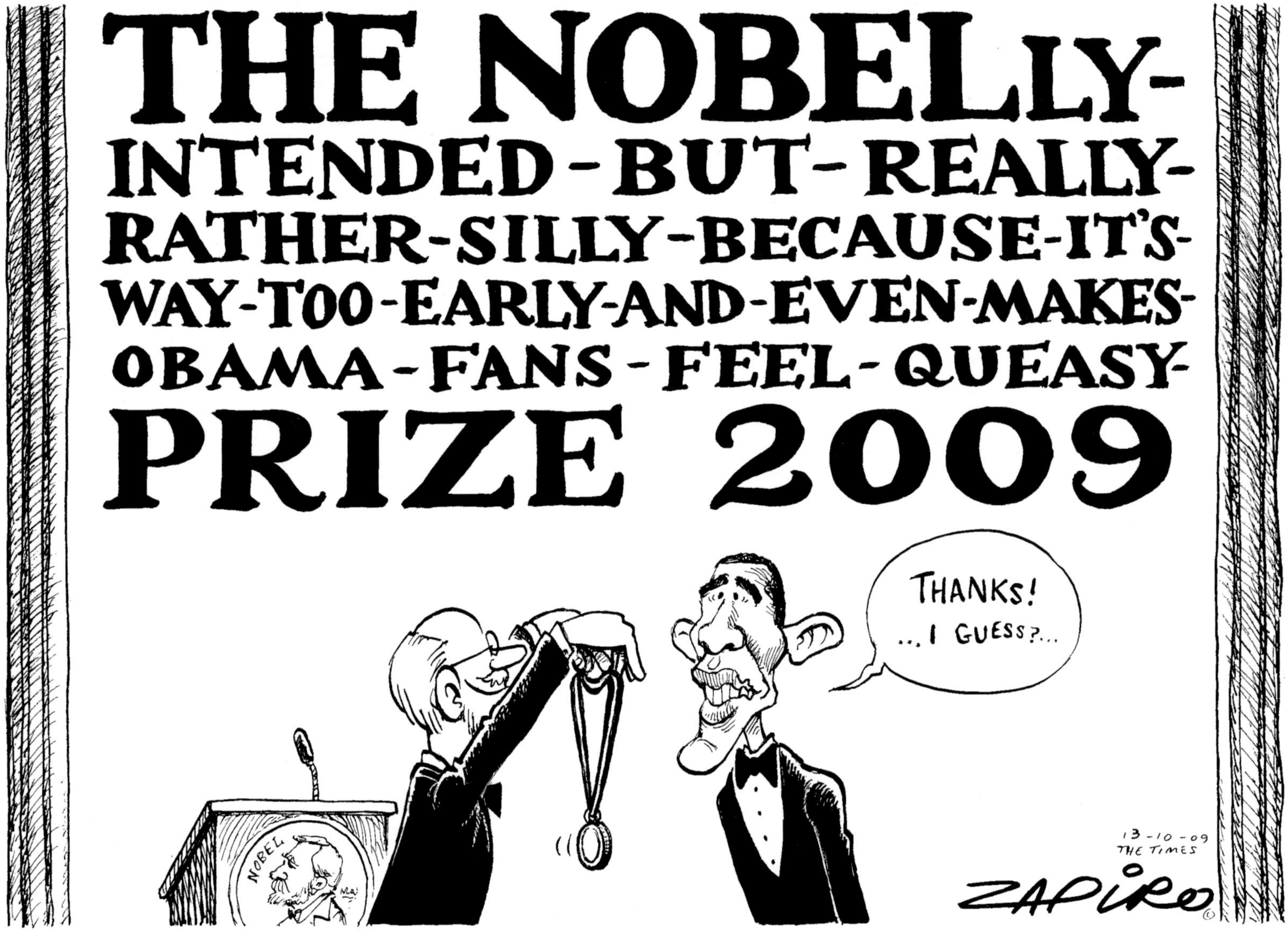
THE NOBELLY-
INTENDED-BUT-REALLY-
RATHER-SILLY-BECAUSE-IT'S-
WAY-TOO-EARLY-AND-EVEN-MAKES-
OBAMA-FANS-FEEL-QUEASY-
PRIZE 2009
THANKS!
...I GUESS?...
NOBEL
13-10-09
THE TIMES
ZAPIRO ©

13 October 2009